My So-Called Life as a Proverbs 31 Wife

My So-Called Life as a Proverbs 31 Wife

Sara Horn

HARVEST HOUSE PUBLISHERS
EUGENE, OREGON

Cover design by Dugan Design Group, Bloomington, Minnesota

Cover illustration © iStockphoto / seanjames

Author photo by Crafts Photography

Published in association with the literary agency of Alive Communications, Inc., 7680 Goddard Street, Suite 200, Colorado Springs, CO 80920. www.alivecommunications.com.

This book contains stories in which the author has changed people's names and some details of their situations in order to protect their privacy.

MY SO-CALLED LIFE AS A PROVERBS 31 WIFE
Copyright © 2011 by Sara Horn
Published by Harvest House Publishers
Eugene, Oregon 97402
www.harvesthousepublishers.com

Library of Congress Cataloging-in-Publication Data
    Horn, Sara, 1977-
    My so-called life as a Proverbs 31 wife / Sara Horn.
       p. cm.
    ISBN 978-0-7369-3941-6 (pbk.)
    ISBN 978-0-7369-4213-3 (eBook)
    1. Horn, Sara, 1977- 2. Wives—Religious life. 3. Wives—Biblical teaching. 4. Bible. O.T. Proverbs XXXI, 10-31—Criticism, interpretation, etc. I Title.
    BV4528.15.H672 2011
    248.8'435—dc22

               2011008129

Printed in the United States of America

12 13 14 15 16 17 18 19 / VP-SK / 10 9 8 7 6 5 4

To Cliff

You remind me often that I have your heart,
So I want you to know that while
I may never learn to iron well
Or vacuum in perfectly straight lines,
While I may still burn quesadillas from time to time
And knit uneven, hole-ridden scarves you mistake for
face masks,
I will always seek to bring you good
And not harm.
It's what one does when one gives the heart away,
And you have had my heart for a very long time.
A treasured gift for which I am very blessed
to say and call you
Husband.
I love you.

Acknowledgments

Books never come about by just one person, and this particular project certainly holds up to that statement. So many people have my gratitude, but a few special folk can't go without being named.

First, my thanks to the Harvest House team—to LaRae Weikert and the editorial board for seeing the vision in the story; to Rod Morris, Editor Incredible, who was so patient and helpful from the first section of edits to the last; and to the rest of the fantastic staff, including Brad Moses and Katie Lane for all your wonderful efforts with this project.

I also must thank my agency, Alive Communications, and my agent, Andrea Heinecke. Thank you so much for representing me and being such a first-class Christian organization.

So many women in my life have played a part in shaping me into who I am today: my mom, Gail Owens, who has prayed for me probably more than I will ever realize and who continues to be one of my biggest supporters; my mother-in-law, Ms. Nancy, who is a great example of love in action; other dear ladies I have known, some for a long time and others for just a short while—Carol McGlothlin, Brenda Pace, Jennifer Cook, Jennifer Schuchmann, Dori Cook, Leighann McCoy, Carol Veneman, Karen Radcliff, and Jackie Lacy. Thank you for your examples.

Thank you to my Wives of Faith ministry leaders and board members—Stephanie, Shauna, Deanna, Leanne (who is also my booking coordinator), Jessica, Pattie, and Tasha. I am daily humbled to be connected with each of you. You exemplify what it means to be women after God's heart, and I am grateful to know you.

The year that I have recorded in these pages has been one of the most severe in terms of winding roads, detours, U-turns, and occasional (and literal) fender benders. I could not have gone through any of it without the love of my life, Cliff Horn. Handsome, you are such a blessing to me in so many ways, and I am so grateful to be your wife. I am so proud of the man you are and the service you give our country alongside the other men and women of our military forces. I am looking forward to the next chapter God writes in this life of ours, and I'm so happy to be doing it by your side.

I end these notes with a grateful prayer of thanksgiving to God:

> *Lord, only you knew how these pages would be written before this whole experiment began, and I am thankful for the lessons you taught me and the changes you've made in my heart and my life. Help me continue to always strive to be the wife and mom you desire for me to be. Amen.*

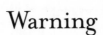

Warning

This book is not a collection of tips on cooking, sewing, and all things homemaking. If that's what you're looking for, please look for another book. If anything, what you hold in your hands might be better described as a collection of what not to do. This book is really just one woman's story of her quest to be a better wife—and what happens when her circumstances don't cooperate.

My experience won't be your experience. But you may see parts of your experience in the pages that follow. You may find yourself challenged with some of the questions I've asked myself. Or, at the very least, you may learn that there's at least one wife out there worse off than you.

I do what I can to help others.

Oh Be Careful
What You Preach

Yesterday was Sunday.

Our pastor started a new sermon series on the family. We missed the first sermon last week, but we were there yesterday for the second. The first week was "Dads Matter More than Anything." This week's was titled "Moms Matter Just as Much."

Good to know.

As the pastor got started, I pulled out my Bible and my notebook, all ready to take notes. But then he said something that made my stomach churn. My hands instinctively made fists. My eyebrows furrowed.

The biblical passage he was speaking from was Proverbs 31.

Of course, I muttered to myself, turning to the passage I revere and fear at the same time.

The Proverbs 31 wife and I don't get along very well. I don't appreciate how bad she makes me look. I don't like the guilt I feel when I see her. If she is the standard all Christian wives should work toward, then I'm in serious trouble. If she's the equivalent of Miss America, then I'm a whole lot more like Lucille Ball. I have a lot of explaining to do for why I'm not more like Miss America. And I'm not really sure I can.

The pastor started making his points:

* An Excellent Wife Is a Rare Find (v. 10).

* An Excellent Wife Can Be Trusted in Every Way (vv. 11-12).

✳ An Excellent Wife Is Concerned for Others (v. 20).

✳ An Excellent Wife Is Strong and Stable (v. 25).

And so it went.

I stopped taking notes at "An Excellent Wife Is a Tireless Worker."

My husband glanced over at me when he heard my notebook snap shut. He knows that's never a good sign. Neither was the steam coming out of my ears and the laser stare in my eyes. He started looking for the exits, just in case.

I don't like it when men tell women what will make us excellent. I don't consider myself a feminist at all, but I just don't think men can possibly understand the woman any more than we can understand the man. That's why *Men Are from Mars, Women Are from Venus* was written. Eve may have been formed from the man's rib, but she definitely had a mind of her own. And maybe, just maybe, if Adam had taken more time to understand her, the whole scene with the apple and the garden might have gone a lot better. Just sayin'.

Part of my struggle with the treatment of the fairer sex comes from the attitudes I've witnessed through the church denomination I've partly grown up and worked in. I agree with a lot that my denomination stands for. But when it comes to the treatment and attitudes about the service of women in the church, it often leaves me with the same feeling I get when I hear fingernails scratch down a chalkboard.

What I don't understand is why there's this 21-verse list of what the perfect wife is and not at least a Top 10 of what makes a perfect husband. I raised this question once on Facebook, and a guy I know who is deep into seminary classes pointed out that Ephesians 5:25-28 is an all-encompassing directive for husbands. See what you think:

> Husbands, love your wives, just as Christ loved the church and gave himself up for her to make her holy, cleansing her by the washing with water through the word, and to present her to himself as a radiant church, without stain or wrinkle or any other blemish, but holy and blameless. In this same way, husbands ought to love their wives as their own bodies. He who loves his wife loves himself.

Really? That's great. Husbands are told to love their wives as they love themselves, and wives are given a laundry list of ways to show our love (just in case we might get confused and think the husband, as part of his love, might also "get up while it's still dark and provide food" for his family). Husbands—you show love. Wives—get to cookin'.

Back to my stewing. I sat, listening to our pastor as he continued to speak on all the things that make an excellent wife, from the example of the Proverbs 31 superwoman:

A wife of noble character who can find?
    She is worth far more than rubies.
Her husband has full confidence in her
    and lacks nothing of value.
She brings him good, not harm,
    all the days of her life.
She selects wool and flax
    and works with eager hands.
She is like the merchant ships,
    bringing her food from afar.
She gets up while it is still night;
    she provides food for her family
    and portions for her female servants.
She considers a field and buys it;
    out of her earnings she plants a vineyard.
She sets about her work vigorously;
    her arms are strong for her tasks.
She sees that her trading is profitable,
    and her lamp does not go out at night.
In her hand she holds the distaff
    and grasps the spindle with her fingers.
She opens her arms to the poor
    and extends her hands to the needy.
When it snows, she has no fear for her household;
    for all of them are clothed in scarlet.
She makes coverings for her bed;
    she is clothed in fine linen and purple.

Her husband is respected at the city gate,
     where he takes his seat among the elders of the land.
She makes linen garments and sells them,
     and supplies the merchants with sashes.
She is clothed with strength and dignity;
     she can laugh at the days to come.
She speaks with wisdom,
     and faithful instruction is on her tongue.
She watches over the affairs of her household
     and does not eat the bread of idleness.
Her children arise and call her blessed;
     her husband also, and he praises her:
"Many women do noble things,
     but you surpass them all."
Charm is deceptive, and beauty is fleeting;
     but a woman who fears the LORD is to be praised.
Honor her for all that her hands have done,
     and let her works bring her praise at the city gate.
          (Proverbs 31:10-31)

I kept reading this passage, over and over, the successes of this great wifely role model taunting me more than encouraging me, my very being wilting and shrinking as I sat there, no comparison to this giant of an example. I was waiting, for what, I didn't know. Waiting for something—a bright glimmer, anything that my pastor might say to give all the wives sitting in the audience, or maybe just me, some hope. He didn't let me down. His last point was the same point I have made in the past: The Proverbs 31 woman's most important task is to fear the Lord (v. 30).

My breathing relaxed a little. This, after all, was something I understood. Of course, I want to be a better wife and homemaker. I want to be a better woman in general. But my greatest desire is to be closer to God as his daughter. I want that close, incredible relationship with him.

I haven't always done well with this. If God and I were going for a walk in the park, I'd be the kid running out in front, barely able to wait for him. Patience is not my strength. Waiting on God is hard.

I began to prayerfully think over the pounding of my heart, the churning of my stomach, and my fingers digging into my thighs. *OK, so why am I so mad? Am I mad at the Proverbs 31 wife? Am I upset with the pastor? Am I angry at myself?* I mean, I argued with myself. *Wouldn't it be great if you COULD be like the Proverbs 31 wife—if you were praying and reading the Bible and really staying in touch with God every day? Couldn't God help you do it all?*

He could if he wanted to, I'm sure. I'm just not convinced he wants me to be able to do it all. I'm not even convinced that the Proverbs 31 wife was real. I mean, I grew up being told King Solomon wrote the book of Proverbs, and he wasn't exactly a role model when it came to women. He liked having as many wives as he could, and in fact it was his infatuation for the opposite sex that got him into trouble toward the end of his reign.

What if this woman we've all idolized and tried to emulate is just a concoction from King Solomon and a group of his royal cronies who sat around one day, drinking beers, and decided to have an impromptu brainstorming session on what makes the perfect wife? And some servant of his wrote all of these ideas down on a big Post-it note and it eventually made its way into Proverbs with all the other wise things Solomon wrote? In fact, my Bible notes that verses 10-31, the Proverbs 31-wife passage, is actually an acrostic. Each verse begins with a successive letter of the Hebrew alphabet. See? I told you it was a drinking game.*

Or if this woman really did exist, then maybe she was like the Martha Stewart of her day, and I'm sure the majority of the women living in that time didn't like her and didn't appreciate her. And while they watched her television shows and read her magazine, *Housekeeping in the Holy Land,* behind closed doors, they lived in fear and guilt that one day their husbands would come home and say, "Why can't you be more like the Proverbs 31 wife?"

But then I got a crazy idea. Why *can't* I be more like the Proverbs 31 wife? What would it be like to try and actually follow the example of this woman so many hold in such esteem?

I definitely had some things to think about.

---

* I've since learned that though most of Proverbs was written or compiled by King Solomon, the work of others was added to his, including Proverbs 30 and 31. So much for my theory.

Beating Egg Whites

After coming home yesterday from church, I was still in deep thought about the whole idea of being a Proverbs 31 wife. I mean, the idea sounds great. Who doesn't want to be organized, who doesn't want to see her family be successful and together and happy? But wanting and doing are two different things.

Still, I agreed with my pastor on at least one point: The wife creates the stability for the home. When mama's not happy, nobody's happy, right? I know this was the case for me growing up, and I know that when things are good for me, they're good for my family. And when they're not…well, maybe that's why my husband and son sometimes disappear.

The Proverbs 31 wife has a happy family, according to verses 28-29:

> Her children arise and call her blessed;
>> her husband also, and he praises her:
> "Many women do noble things,
>> but you surpass them all."

Who doesn't want her kids to like her so much they bless her or actually pay her a compliment? Who doesn't want her husband praising her and going on and on about how great the house looks and how good dinner was?

I still felt antsy about this topic, so I did what I always do when I'm stressed. I cleaned. The kitchen was a wreck, with papers and odds and ends from my son's first week of the school year all thrown haphazardly onto the counter. The sink sat full of dishes, and the stovetop hadn't been cleaned in days and stains around the burners had lingered for weeks and weeks. My husband is a great cook, much better than I am, but not so great at cleaning. I'm good at cleaning, just not so great at making time for it.

As I put some things away, I noticed the messy pantry, not to be outdone by the similarly disorganized fridge, so I spent about two hours reorganizing everything. I pulled things out, I put things back. I tossed old veggies that were past their prime. I moved cake- and cookie-decorating stuff out of drawers and into a nearby closet, since I don't use them very often.

Then I tackled the stove using a baking-powder paste, one of the few tricks I learned from a Mary Hunt book I read many years ago. While the white gooey stuff sat absorbing the stains, I pulled out my laptop and went to our church's website. I wanted to be fair to our pastor, so I decided to listen to his first sermon I had missed, the one titled "Dads Matter More than Anything."

I couldn't help but notice how different the points were compared to the second week. For the men, my pastor had these points:

* Pure Motives
* Approved by God
* Not Men Pleasers
* Not Greedy
* Gentle with People
* Filled with Love

(And to review) For the women, my pastor had these points:

* An Excellent Wife Is a Rare Find
* An Excellent Wife Can Be Trusted in Every Way
* An Excellent Wife Is a Tireless Worker
* An Excellent Wife Is Concerned for Others

* An Excellent Wife Is Strong and Stable
* An Excellent Wife Is Full of Wisdom
* An Excellent Wife Fears the Lord

So if men are supposed to be the leaders of the home, are women supposed to be the workhorses? Because it sure looks that way on paper. I mean, the men didn't even get complete sentences for their topics, more like the Cliff Notes version. The topics for women, on the other hand, left very little room for guessing.

I took my frustration out on the stains covered with the baking-powder paste. My confidence grew as I watched much of the brown crackled stains slowly fade with the more elbow grease I used.

The sermon ended about the same time I finished the stove scrubbing chore. I surveyed my work and noticed the satisfaction I felt. Maybe I could try doing this Proverbs 31 wife thing for a little while. Maybe. But I would need to take baby steps. I couldn't jump into adopting all twenty-one characteristics at once. I would need to work them in just a few at a time.

While I thought about it, I pulled up a banana pudding recipe on my iPhone. We had vanilla wafers, and my husband had brought bananas back from the store (wonder what Proverbs 31 Wife would think about her hubby grocery shopping?), and I'd told him I would make banana pudding since I know he likes it and I was feeling all domestic in a rebellious sort of way.

The only problem was I couldn't find a recipe using instant pudding. Yes, I'm that kind of cook. A shortcut, instant kind of cook. Not very patient. And the whole double boiler idea made me nervous. Still, my pride was on the line. I needed to show Proverbs 31 Wife that she wasn't the only one who could "provide food for her family" (v. 15).

The recipe called for sugar, two cups of milk, three egg yolks, and a little flour to be placed in the top pot while the one underneath boiled water. But when I went to crack the eggs, I was a little confused. Normally, the few times I have separated eggs, I save the egg whites. I glanced again at the recipe. Nope, didn't look like I needed the whites for anything. I resisted my urge to save them anyway, since I had no idea what I would use them for. So, instead of breaking the eggs over a bowl with the separator, I just did it straight over the sink, keeping the yellow yolks and washing the rest down the drain.

The water was boiling. I added the top pot and grabbed a wooden spoon from the nearest drawer. I'd read somewhere it was good to use a wooden spoon instead of metal—whether it applied to this situation, I had no idea. Still, I felt domestically smart. I set a timer on my microwave for ten minutes. The instructions said to "stir constantly" and that's what I did. I have a bad habit of putting something on the stove and then wandering away to check email or grab a book. Twenty minutes later I usually remember what I was doing.

So this time, I hovered. I stirred. I paid attention to my egg/sugar/flour/milk concoction. No books for me. No email checking. Around the seven-minute mark, I noticed the consistency had started to thicken. Should I take it off now? I couldn't decide, so I just waited for the timer to go off. I pulled the top pot off and placed it on a cool burner and turned the other burner off.

Next I had to cut up the bananas and pull out the vanilla wafers. It occurred to me that I might have needed to do this before I actually started cooking. I was still worried the custard-looking stuff might burn or get lumpy, so in between banana slices, I pulled the wooden spoon around a couple of times in the pot. Just to be safe.

After I layered the vanilla wafers, banana slices, and pudding in the bowl, I took another look at the recipe. Add the remaining sugar to the egg whites…Crud. Apparently I'd missed that little line. So what to do? Skip it? Put the banana pudding in the oven without the meringue? Or waste three more eggs?

Reasoning that my husband had just bought a couple more dozen eggs because they'd been on sale and it was okay if I used three more, I went with the last choice. And this time watched three yolks go down the drain.

The instructions said I needed to "Beat egg whites until stiff peaks form." Well, I had no idea what stiff peaks looked like, but I vowed I was going to do it. I grabbed my whisk and started stirring. Hmmm… this was taking a while. I stirred some more. *I wonder if the whisk is the right tool to use? Might it prevent the egg whites from thickening in some way?* I grabbed a spoon. Kept stirring. *This is taking a really long time…* After a while my arm started hurting. Which made me think of the verse in Proverbs 31 that says "her arms are strong for her tasks." *I wonder if Proverbs 31 Wife worked out at the gym?* I made a mental note that I might have to do just that.

I finally noticed some bubbling and the egg whites seemed to get a little whiter. After adding the sugar, I went back to stirring. Faster and faster. Talking to myself in my head. *Maybe I should use the mixer. NO! I'm sure the Proverbs 31 wife wouldn't! Yeah, but if she'd had one, would she? She was resourceful, after all.*

Convinced she probably would use a mixer had she lived two thousand years from when she actually did, I grabbed mine but attached only one wire whip instead of two (as though using only one was like being only a little pregnant—I was cheating only a little). I turned it on high and promptly watched drops of egg white go everywhere, including all over my laptop. So I backed it down to a slower setting and watched to see if any peaks formed. After ten minutes, I finally started seeing meringuish-looking foamy stuff. The instructions called for "stiff but not dry," and not wanting to take any chances, I stopped. I spooned the egg whites over the pudding and stuck it in the oven.

Once it cooked for a bit and there were nice little bits of brown on the meringue, I took it out and stuck it in the fridge to let it cool. By this time, I'd made my decision. Maybe I could do it. What did I have to lose? I would attempt to follow the Proverbs 31 wife.

Then I started getting dinner ready. KFC leftovers from lunch that I popped in the microwave.

Like I said, baby steps.

Shrimp and Pasta

I started thinking yesterday. You know, Proverbs 31 Wife needs a name. What I mean is, if I'm going to be writing about her, the least I can do is actually refer to her by name rather than some nameless general term like "the Proverbs 31 wife." So since I picture her as the biblical Martha Stewart, I think that's what I'll call her—Martha. But just to make sure I don't get her confused with the more modern, contemporary Martha of today (or the biblical Martha from the story of Mary, Martha, and Lazarus), I'll call her Martha 31.

Yesterday was a good day as Mondays go. My husband had a couple of meetings with the company he's been doing some freelance marketing for, and then he called to let me know he was meeting a buddy for lunch who then asked him to come over to his office and help out with an afternoon job.

Cliff and I met three days after I graduated from high school when my family moved from Pennsylvania to Louisiana, to a small town where we lived during my late elementary and middle school years. A friend of ours from my family's old church invited some of the college guys to help move us into our new house, and Cliff and his twin brother had agreed to be part of the welcoming committee (at least after their dad mentioned there were daughters in the family). But I never saw his brother that day. Despite driving all night without getting a shower, I guess I managed to clean up enough not to scare Cliff away, because once we saw each other, it seemed we were never apart.

I remembered talking with him that first day and noticing his dark hazel eyes and his great smile that flashed when he was cracking a joke, which he did often. The next day, I ran into him again in town, and he invited me over to his family's house to watch movies with some friends. We spent almost every day together after that, and my parents warned me about tying myself down before I left for college just a month later.

But it was too late. I was hooked, and after dating mostly long-distance for a year and a half, Cliff proposed on Christmas Day, and we married in June of 1998. We've been married for twelve years as I write this, and time has flown by, especially after our son was born.

But our happy marriage hasn't been without its challenges. Cliff has been out of work now for more than a year, and we are definitely in a "down" season. He's a Navy reservist, and six months after he got back from his first deployment to Iraq, his position at the nonprofit where he worked was eliminated. He has struggled to find another full-time job, and I have trouble sometimes with resentment and thinking if he only did this or if he only did that, he would have a job by now.

It's also been an adjustment having him home all the time. Cliff has a lot of wonderful qualities, but I would not consider self-discipline and assertiveness to be in that list. I often feel as if I'm working for both of us, trying to keep myself going as a freelance writer and then trying to encourage him to do…whatever. At least he doesn't lie around and watch television. He's also a fantastic cook and a great dad to our son.

So he was gone for most of yesterday, working on a freelance project for a company in town, and I was a little glad he was. It's nice sometimes to have the mental space and be alone.

I told myself earlier that day that I would start dinner before Cliff got home. I confess I can be really bad at this, especially if I'm working upstairs in our office. I can be a workaholic, and it's hard sometimes to pull myself away from the computer when I'm in the middle of something. I wonder if Martha 31 ever had this problem. The passage tells us she was, after all, a business woman as well as a great wife and mother. How did she juggle it all?

So after I picked up our son from school and we came home, I decided to stay downstairs with Caleb, talking about his day at school and getting stuff out for dinner. On Sunday, we sat down as a family and reviewed what meals we would have this week and when. Monday night was shrimp pasta Florentine, an idea I found from a group of recipes in my *Women's Health* magazine. Cliff had taken out the frozen shrimp that morning to thaw, but as I reviewed the recipe that afternoon, I realized it called for something we didn't have. Fettuccine Alfredo frozen entrees. These recipes are all supposed to be semi-healthy and fast to make because you take something that's already cooked and add to it to make it better. I also saw we didn't have the baby spinach we needed.

Normally, I admit, my tendency at that point in the dinner-making process would be to A) scrap the whole idea and order pizza or B) call up Cliff and ask him to pick up the items we needed, which always makes dinner much later. But I thought about what Martha 31 might do, and I just decided to grab my keys and my son and head to the grocery store. Within fifteen minutes we were back with the fettuccine and two bags of baby spinach, enough to add to the lasagna rolls we're having tomorrow night. (Cliff asked for the lasagna rolls, and since I want to "bring him good, not harm" (31:12), of course he can have lasagna rolls even though we're already having a pasta dish tonight.)

My biggest dilemma though was trying to figure out when exactly to start dinner. That evening we had our son's parent open house with his third-grade teacher, so I knew I'd have to make sure we timed it all just right. I called Cliff to see when he thought he might be home. I had to be careful with this phone call because my usual tendency is to get irritated if he doesn't come home on time, and since he was working on a project, I didn't know when he would be close to finishing.

"Hey!" I said, trying to sound nonchalant when he answered the phone. I could hear guys laughing in the background. Cliff was doing freelance work for a small agency he's worked for before—they do a lot of web marketing and promotion and most of the guys there are single programmer-types. I heard Cliff laugh and jokingly say "quit…shut up" to someone. I figured he was getting razzed about the little wifey calling, so I didn't say anything, just launched into why I'd called.

"Hey, just calling to see when you think you might be home. I'm trying to figure out when to have dinner ready."

More laughter and noise in the background. I was starting to feel bad about interrupting his fun.

"Um...I'm gonna try to leave here by 5:00," Cliff said.

I did a quick tally in my head with the distance and rush hour traffic. "So that puts you here at 5:40 or so?" I said.

"Yeah, is that OK?"

"That works," I said. "See you when you get home."

More laughter and more razzing as I heard his phone hang up. Men.

This gave me a little bit of a dilemma. Since we were using these frozen entrees, it wasn't going to take long to get dinner ready. But we've been trying to keep the television off since we had a "no television" week last week, and I was really trying to keep my new third grader focused and not distracted. We had about thirty minutes, so we decided to go on a walk and take the dog.

On the way back, I ran into my neighbor Rachel who was standing outside. Rachel would definitely fit into the Proverbs 31 wife club if there was one (which I'm sure there is; I just haven't been invited). Her house is always spotless and her family rarely eats out—she's always cooking, and new recipes at her house aren't the special occasion, they're the norm. Her kids are all in college, though living at home, and she doesn't work. She does a great job at shopping and using coupons and finding deals. She once brought us over six boxes of mac 'n' cheese (the blue box kind) because she'd bought them for free.

Talking with her on the street now, however, I started getting nervous and looking at my watch. Conversing with Rachel is always fun but it's never short. And I really wanted to make sure I had dinner ready before Cliff got home. By the time I started walking in, I had twenty minutes. We were going to be cutting it close.

The fact I was actually nervous about getting supper on the table before my husband got home made me wonder what this little experiment, short as it's been so far, has already done to my thinking. I have never wanted or thought of myself as the happy housewife kind. So scrambling to set dishes on the table and get it all plated is a new feeling for me.

But I have to admit, the dish I made last night was fun. I had to add a few dabs of garlic, spinach leaves, and the frozen shrimp to a skillet. The only setback was that the shrimp Cliff bought from the store were cocktail shrimp, which still had the tails on them. And they weren't completely thawed. So I stood at the counter, holding frozen shrimp over a bowl, quickly pulling ice and tails off while ignoring the numbing cold seeping through my fingertips. It took a lot longer than I thought.

Then, when I added the bag of baby spinach, I decided it was way too much. We are gradually adding vegetables to our family's diet, but I knew that amount of green might send our eight-year-old over the edge. I took half the spinach out, but since it had touched the shrimp and I wasn't sure if it was contaminated, I threw it away. Yes, more wasted food to go with my egg yolks and egg whites from yesterday.

Once the skillet began sizzling and the third individual entree of fettuccine was in the microwave (the frozen entree is the way to cook, by the way, whether Martha 31 would do it that way or not), I quickly got the table set and glasses out for drinks. I had to cook the shrimp, baby spinach, and garlic until the spinach leaves started wilting, and I wasn't really sure what that looked like until it actually started happening. The leaves started getting darker green and shrinking up a bit. Then it was time to dump the fettuccine in and mix it all up. Dinner was ready.

Just then, Cliff walked in.

"Wow!" I heard him say as he came in through the garage and across the living room. "That smells *really* good."

Dinner went well, and even the eight-year-old ate everything on his plate.

> Her children arise, and call her blessed;
> her husband also, and he praises her:
> "Many women do noble things,
> but you surpass them all."
> (Proverbs 31:28-29)

It's a little thing, shrimp and pasta, but it's a start.

I Never Wanted to
Be a Homemaker

Getting married, for me, was never with the goal of staying home, raising 2.2 children, and decorating my house with the white picket fence. It just meant I'd get to see my best friend daily and do life with him. It actually used to drive me crazy for Cliff to stumble upon me doing something "homey," like baking bread or attempting to sew a button back on, and hear him call me, in an endearing tone, his "little homemaker." He meant nothing demeaning by it; in fact, he really loved seeing me in moments like that, just as much as he loved seeing me score another book deal or finish dreaming up another website to create.

I, for the record, however, didn't *want* to be a "homemaker." Homemakers were women who never went to college, or if they did, they had thrown all of that promise and potential for success away to spend time changing diapers and baking cookies and scrapbooking. Homemakers, in my experience, weren't always happy. They could get angry and tired of picking up toys and making dinner, and instead of playing with the kids, they yelled at the kids.

I still remember being on maternity leave, at home with Caleb in the little apartment we lived in off the university campus where I worked, and listening to the stay-at-home mom below us scream at her children—constantly. I never wanted to be like that and vowed during that time that I never would.

Don't get me wrong, changing diapers and baking cookies and scrapbooking are all great things—I've done all of those things, including the scrapbooking, but it was always in the mix of other ambitions and dreams. Eventually I had to give up the scrapbooking because, like a lot of things in my life, it became a challenge to overcome or to find perfection in instead of just something fun to do to relax. But those weren't the only things I wanted to do.

When I met Cliff, my goal was to sing. I'd used all my graduation money to put together a little demo tape, and I'd earned a music scholarship for college. One day, I just knew I would go to Nashville and sing Christian music. But as Cliff and I got more serious, I became disenchanted with the music degree I was studying for. I was sick of and just plain bored with classical music (what all music majors train in), and I started finding opportunities to focus more and more on communications—writing articles, working in radio, dabbling in public relations. Still, my dream was to sing and do concerts.

"You know, if you get married, you're not going to be able to travel and do concerts," my mother told me one day.

I was home from school for the summer, Cliff was away at boot camp, and I was mooning over bridal magazines as I did just about daily.

"Why not?" I asked, my nose turned up at what my mother was suggesting.

"Because you'll have your own family and you'll need to be there for your husband and for your kids, if and when you ever have any," she said. "You're not going to be able to travel everywhere and still have a family."

Looking back, I know my mom had good intentions—maybe she said it to make me think about whether music was really my calling, or maybe she said it to make me think about whether I really loved Cliff enough to give up my music. Regardless, it was the first time I'd ever been forced to face the fact I might actually have to choose between marital bliss and pursuing a dream.

And she wasn't the only one who suggested I couldn't follow a dream and still get married. Later, back at school, after Cliff and I'd announced our engagement, the director of the seven-member student vocal group I sang in stunned me one day when he announced that I wouldn't be allowed to be part of the group once I was married. "You'll need to focus on your marriage, not traveling around with us," he told me (a guy, I might add, who *wasn't* married). I became angry, both with my mom and with my director, and I remember thinking, *Why can't I do both?* Particularly with my director, it annoyed me that someone else would decide for me whether I could or couldn't handle following a dream while being a wife. It was almost as if becoming a wife meant giving up any other part of me. But I really begged to disagree. And I was even more determined that it wouldn't happen.

I certainly had no intention of being a wife who stayed at home, whatever that meant.

But God had other plans in mind for me than singing, and through a couple of very specific events, he led me into a writing career, which I immediately took on and ran with, looking for opportunities to advance and find what I interpreted as success.

For years I worked, and I worked hard. I piled on the work and at twenty-six years old, I was working a forty-hour corporate writing job, finishing up my bachelor's degree, and writing my first book after taking two trips to the Middle East. Oh, and when I wasn't trying to save the world, I was a wife and a mom to our two-year-old. Another goal of mine that didn't happen by accident but by choice. A year after we married, I got a bad case of baby fever. I saw babies everywhere. And soon, we decided to have our own. At the time, I thought of having a child and being a parent as a great accomplishment, but it wasn't the only accomplishment I wanted. There were so many other things I wanted to achieve. So I was busy. And I got busier.

Being busy made me feel good. Being busy made me feel important. Back then I said I was just driven—I loved making a difference. Today I would say I had my priorities seriously out of whack. But my patient husband took it all in stride, and at night after Caleb fell asleep, while I worked on a chapter for my book, he would kneel on the floor or sit at the table in our small apartment kitchen, setting up one of the many physics experiments I needed to do for the online physics course I was taking.

Maybe I've mellowed some in my now thirty-something years, but I'm no longer as resistant to the idea of being a homemaker. Now, I actually worry that I've missed out. That I'm behind the learning curve. I mean, there are very few things I cook well. And while I can clean when I put my mind to it, I'm not the neatest housekeeper. And I have no idea how to sew. (I attempted it once, sewing a Bob the Tomato costume for Caleb when he was two, which came out looking like a pretty decent facsimile but would not have won any seamstress awards.) I worry that I have been so swept up in career that I forgot to pay attention to home.

I'd really like to change that.

Getting Started

So I've been wondering how I can start to really follow what Martha 31 does. I mean, if you look at all twenty-one verses, that's a big tall order to take on all at once. I think the best way to handle it is to break some of the verses up and tackle a few at a time. Since I have a year, I don't need to try and do it all in a week. I'm pretty sure that would be impossible. At least for me.

I thought the first thing I could try is what the first few verses say:

> A wife of noble character who can find?
>   She is worth far more than rubies.
> Her husband has full confidence in her
>   and lacks nothing of value.
> She brings him good, not harm,
>   all the days of her life.
> (Proverbs 31:10-12)

I also looked it up in The Message version, which uses a more contemporary wording:

> A good woman is hard to find,
>   and worth far more than diamonds.
> Her husband trusts her without reserve,
>   and never has reason to regret it.
> Never spiteful, she treats him generously
>   all her life long.

I'm not sure I'm always a good woman to my husband. OK, I'm pretty sure I'm not. I want to be—I try to be—but my temper or my impatience or my "he should do it this way (my way!)" sometimes, uh, gets in the way.

I looked up the word *spiteful*—it means vengeful, mean, cruel, rancorous. I don't think I'm spiteful, at least to that degree. I can be fussy, I can be grumpy.

Let's look at what *spiteful* doesn't mean. The antonym is *benevolent*. "Characterized by or expressing goodwill or kind feelings." Gentle, good, gracious, kind, goodhearted, merciful, obliging...

Oh boy. How often do I show "goodwill" to my husband? Not a whole lot. I mean, a genuine eagerness to be kind and show kindness specifically for the sake or purpose of being kind and showing goodwill to my husband?

I usually get so caught up with my work, with the things I'm doing, that this is an area I don't do so well in.

I think to help me get a good start on it, I'm going to need reinforcements. If you saw the movie *Fireproof*, you remember the book that Kirk Cameron's character used, *The Love Dare*. Cliff actually bought the book before we went and saw the movie. I kept waiting for him to use it. I think he did two days of it.

So maybe it's time for me to use it. I think it lasts for about forty days. Surely that's enough time for me to learn what it means to bring Cliff good and not harm, benevolence and not spite.

Need to look for the book. It's around here somewhere.

* * *

Yesterday I found *The Love Dare* sitting where it's sat I think for the last year, on top of Cliff's dresser. I slipped it out from under a couple of other books and took it up to my office while he was out of the house, dropping off our son at school and working out at the gym.

The first day is patience. Hmmm. Not so great at patience. And not so great when it comes to patience and my hubby.

If there's one skill that Cliff does well (and don't get me wrong, he has many), he can describe things in extreme detail and hold onto random facts the way pregnant women hold water. It's just there! And every once in a while, it has to come out. But I'm not always patient about this. Especially when it's about some techno toy or a movie like *GI Joe* that he and Caleb went to and they tried to tell me about in the car the other day. I could feel the glaze forming over my eyeballs.

But my goal right now is to follow the Proverbs 31 wife, I mean Martha 31, and to be a wife of noble character, a wife who brings my husband good, not harm. And that, according to *The Love Dare*, starts with patience.

Yesterday wasn't bad as patience goes. We both spent most of the day working at our computers. Then Cliff couldn't find a power cord for his external hard drive. And I braced myself.

"Hey, have you seen a power cord?"

Normally, this drives me crazy. Who deemed it that moms and wives should know all and be able to find all that is lost? I have no idea where his power cord is. Nor do I really want to stop and help look. But I take a deep breath. Patience.

"No, when did you have it last?" I said, trying to keep my voice calm and pleasant.

He didn't know.

Patience.

"Did you check the cabinet? Did you look in your bag?"

And then he was standing by my desk. Hovering. Because of course his power cord is probably on my desk. Makes sense, right?

"It looks like yours…" he said.

But I had bigger concerns. *The Love Dare* was sitting right there, just a foot in front of him in the top drawer of the side cabinet I use for storage. His fingers were just inches away, and I knew if he opened that drawer, he'd see the book and it would be all over. (OK, knowing my husband, he probably would not have thought anything of it; but still, I didn't want to take the chance.) Nothing like trying to work on being a better wife when your husband knows you're trying to. Doesn't really have the same result, does it?

But I was trying to practice patience, and so if I snapped at him or tried to shoo him away, I'd fail what I'd set out to do for the day.

His fingers touched the handle of the drawer as he scanned the stuff on top of it. There he went—slowly pulling it open...

"Hey honey, I don't think it's in there," I said, trying to keep my voice steady as his hand stopped after pulling the drawer about an inch out. "Is it in the bottom one?"

Of course, this didn't make any sense, since the bottom drawer is all hanging file folders, but hey, it kept him from looking in the top drawer. He finally went on to look somewhere else, and I resisted a big sigh of relief.

The rest of the day was uneventful for the most part. I made a point to go downstairs and get us lunch, which I think surprised Cliff. Usually he's the one who does it, because I'm always so into whatever I'm doing at the moment I don't want to stop, and we both would starve (or at least I would) if someone didn't stop and go make lunch.

I pulled out the shrimp and pasta we'd had the night before, arranged it nicely on plates, and added rolls I'd warmed up in the oven and added butter to. After we ate, I cleared away the dishes (we ate at our desks) and offered to bring him some leftover banana pudding, which he happily accepted.

When I got home after picking Caleb up from school, Cliff was already downstairs, and we started working on dinner—open-faced chicken tacos. It was a joint effort tonight, and since Cliff was intent on making the taco filling, I did the other stuff—getting drinks ready, table set, and helping Caleb with his homework.

After dinner, we got ready to go to Caleb's first Cub Scout pack meeting. I totally didn't suspect this is where my patience would truly be tested. I'm not sure if it was organized chaos or disorganized chaos since I'm not that familiar with the Cub Scouts, but the noise level in the school cafeteria almost drove me up the wall.

My husband, Cool Hand Cliff (and former Boy Scout), was fine with it. I tried to reason with myself that I could be impatient with the scouts and still be patient with my hubby. Overall, it went OK, though I do think I came close to showing some moments of impatience, such as when one of the brothers of a scout decided to pitch *the* Mother of all Tantrums right there where the parents all sat, screaming as loud as he could.

Also, speaking of screaming, did you know that boys can squeal just like girls? I'm pretty sure of it now, because I definitely heard squealing last night, and yet all I saw were about thirty boys.

My one reward from the day came at the end of the night. I finished reading the book Caleb and I were reading together, tucked him into bed, and after nearly falling asleep in Caleb's room, joined Cliff in our bed. He pulled me close.

"The last couple of days have been really good," he murmured.

"Yeah?"

"Yeah, it seems like you've gotten yourself on a schedule. You aren't staying up in the office so much like you usually do."

I smiled in the dark, happy to know that my efforts (so far) were paying off.

Cliff chuckled. "Of course, it's only Tuesday."

The Kindness of
a Proverbs 31 Wife

I don't think the Proverbs 31 wife ever had deadlines.

I mean, maybe she did. I guess she probably did, since we're told "she makes linen garments and sells them, and supplies the merchants with sashes" (v. 24).

But I really would like to know how she did it and everything else.

Yesterday the "Love Dare" for the day was kindness. Besides being patient, I needed to show kindness as well. I knew the day was going to be a tough one when I got ready to get into the shower. No towels. Cliff, who started the laundry on Monday, still had not finished the laundry, and we had no clean towels in our bathroom.

So I headed over to our son's bathroom to grab one of his. *No towels.* Apparently, the three of us were very dirty last week, because we used every single towel we own. And they were all lying in a pile outside the laundry room door.

Normally, this would have been my signal to complain. If you start the laundry, you need to finish the laundry. And my husband does finish the laundry—it just takes him all week, and by the time it's finished, guess what? Yep, there's another pile of laundry to do.

But yesterday I was supposed to practice patience. And kindness. So I kept my mouth shut. Calmly picked up two (dirty) towels from the pile outside the laundry room door. Went and took my shower.

The whole dirty-towel experience got me thinking. This is what I struggle with when it comes to Martha 31. If she "speaks with wisdom, and faithful instruction is on her tongue" (v. 26), or as the NLT puts it, "she gives instructions with kindness," did she give instructions to her husband? Did he do what she asked? Did he listen to what she said?

Because I have to say, yesterday felt a lot like rolling over and becoming June Cleaver, putting everything and everyone else before myself. Not necessarily a bad thing to do, but I'll get to why it was hard in a minute.

One of the reasons I've struggled so much with the idea of the Proverbs 31 wife is, in part, because of an experience I had in my old job as a writer for a large Christian publishing company. This company has two retreat centers, one on the East Coast and one on the West, and as a corporate writer, I attended and reported on some of the retreats and conferences that were held every year. One of those was a homeschooling retreat.

I would venture to say a lot of aspiring Martha 31s are homeschooling moms. But one specific homeschooling mom pretty much convinced me I never wanted to homeschool. She had seven kids under the age of thirteen, and she homeschooled them all. She did everything—the house, the kids, the schooling, the laundry, the cleaning, even the yard work. She worked herself almost to death to take care of and support her husband.

She described to me how after the birth of her seventh child, she noticed she felt weaker than normal. She found herself waking up before the sun came up (her usual time), and it was all she could do to drag herself across the floor to the bathroom. She didn't tell her husband what was happening (and apparently he was blind), and it was almost too late when she finally did. After seeing a doctor and being ordered to rest in bed, for months, she finally got better, and her husband told me when I interviewed him that he was now helping with dinner a couple of times a week. (Wow, what a big sacrifice he was making.)

Even as she told this story, though, she was still doing most of the work for her family and her husband. They were trying to make different choices, but the concept still was the same—she was the worker bee. He did, well, what he wanted.

So, as I got out of the shower and thought about that, it made me wonder, how far was I willing to go to show love and support to my family and my husband? Enough to find myself dragging across the floor to the bathroom one day? I'm not so sure…

* * *

Yesterday was about kindness, and I did my best to be kind to Cliff. I went and had lunch with a new friend, an Air Force wife whose husband is overseas for a one-year stint in Korea. When I started to head back, I called Cliff to see if he wanted me to bring him something for lunch. Since I was just a minute from the house, it wasn't exactly on my way, but I didn't mind.

He asked me to stop by one of our favorite sandwich places, and I made sure I got exactly everything he wanted on his sub. I ran in, arranged it nicely on a plate (instead of just bringing him the bag), and even added some chips to it and brought him a drink.

Then it was time for me to work. I have two deadlines I'm behind on. Because I'm trying to stop working after our son gets home so I can be downstairs to help him with homework and get dinner started, I'm noticing that time is not my friend. And my workload is high. Normally, I'm pretty demanding that I get to do my work and Cliff gets to do dinner. Since he isn't working a full-time job and he's home most days, I don't think I'm being too unreasonable. But this week I'm trying to be patient and kind, and I'm pretty sure Martha 31 would not tell her husband to get dinner on the table.

But it's caused me a dilemma. Because I have deadlines and commitments. And I'm not sure how I can do everything, especially as aptly as Martha 31 appears to be able to do it.

I got started on my work, trying to track down some experts and a little bit of new information for an article I've already turned in to my editor, but it needed a little something more. Cliff even offered to help me, and after he showed me a paragraph of information he found online that I was happy to see I could use, that's when it happened.

"It's 3:00. Time to go get Caleb."

"Uh-huh," I said. My stomach sank since I was (finally) getting into what I needed to do.

But I was being patient, and I was being kind.

"Want me to go get him, I guess?" I said, holding my breath in hopes he'd say…

"Yes, please."

Not what I was hoping to hear.

I think a sigh must have slipped out because Cliff quickly said, "But I can go do it."

"No, I'll go do it."

After all, I'm putting my husband first, right? Deadlines be damned, I suppose.

I made a point to give him a kiss before I left. And forced a smile. He smiled back. My writing career may go down the tubes, but hey, I'll have a husband who loves me. And I know Cliff loves me. I would venture to say he has almost always loved me unconditionally, from the day we first said our vows. I'm the one who hasn't done so well in that department. Of course, not sure how that translates to money in the bank to pay for everything…

After getting back from the car line, I started working on dinner. Lasagna rolls. The most complicated thing I know how to cook. I know, that's not saying much. It takes a good thirty to forty minutes to prepare and an hour to cook. And we had no cream cheese, which I needed for the filling.

Normally I would say, "Cliff…can you please go get…?"

But instead, I just picked up my purse and said, "OK, I need to run to the store. We forgot to get cream cheese."

"I'll go do it," Cliff said.

Bless him.

So he and Caleb ran to the store, and I worked on mixing the rest of the ingredients for the filling and boiled the whole-wheat lasagna noodles. Once the guys got back, with the missing ingredient as well as some Texas toast, they worked on Caleb's math homework while I worked on the lasagna rolls. After laying out the strips of noodles and letting them cool a bit, I painted on the ricotta-and-cream-cheese mixture and rolled up each noodle and added it to a pan. Pasta sauce over that and cheese over that. Then into the oven for fifty minutes.

By the time I got ready to pull the lasagna out, both Cliff and Caleb had disappeared upstairs. I was talking with a friend on the phone about some plans we had, and opened the oven to pull out the lasagna. *Oh no!* The cheese had burned completely. Not saying anything to my friend, I finished up my conversation with her and surveyed the damage.

My normal inclination would be to pitch a fit. Throw it all out. Proclaim once again how bad a cook I am. And refuse to ever cook a meal again. Somehow, though, I'm pretty sure Martha 31 wouldn't do that.

So I calmly took a fork and pulled off a section of the burnt cheese. Luckily, it came off very easily. I quickly took off the entire layer and threw it away, then added the remaining shredded cheese I had and let that melt on top without putting it back into the oven. Got the Texas toast started. Stuck the lasagna in again the last five minutes so the cheese would melt a bit more. It was all good.

Both Cliff and Caleb liked the meal, and I noticed something. Cliff made a whole lot more compliments. Usually, if I'm lucky, he will say something once. But he said it at least three or four times during the meal.

"This is really, really good."

"This is great. You did a really good job."

"Thanks for making dinner. It's delicious."

To which I replied, "You're welcome. Thanks for doing dishes."

He chuckled, because that's the line he usually gives me. And he did do the dishes. Not sure if Martha 31 would approve, but Martha 31 probably wasn't as tired as I was.

Kindness day went OK, though I probably could have done more. After 7:00, all three of us sat down and watched TV, and after Caleb went to bed, Cliff and I watched two hours of *Top Chef.* I felt a little guilty because I probably should have been upstairs working. I'm still not sure how to balance all of it. I hope I can figure it out.

One thing I am figuring out, though, is what I'm calling the Softness Factor. The softer and nicer I am to my husband, the softer and nicer he is to me. And that, I think, is worth the missed or late deadlines.

Maybe?

Climbing Ladders

For a long time, work was my identity. That may sound odd for a woman to say. Most of the time men are identified with that trait. It always made me feel funny, but when we got together with "couple friends," I usually had more things to talk about with the husbands than with the wives. The men were more inclined to talk about work as I was, and the wives were more apt to talk about shopping, one of my least favorite things to talk about.

After Cliff and I married, we lived for one year in the town where we'd met and where both sets of our parents lived, before we decided it was time to go back to school. While Cliff had an associate's degree from a small community college in Mississippi, I'd spent a year away from school after my sophomore year to work in radio and figure out exactly what I wanted to do after I'd burned out studying classical music. Cliff and I decided to go back to the first school I'd attended, a Baptist university in Tennessee. I'd loved it there but left to transfer to another school in Mississippi to be closer to him after we got serious. The university had added a communications emphasis to their music program, which meant I wouldn't have to completely change majors, wasting the credits I'd already earned.

Being married and living in married-student housing, we both needed jobs. Cliff went to work part-time at the local Sears while he pursued finishing his bachelor of science in business administration; I applied to work in the university relations office. Natalie, the news director, seemed a bit taken aback when I dropped off a resume and writing sample with my student worker application. I suppose she didn't have a lot of college students who thought to do that. But I was determined to open a door to a writing job and didn't want to leave anything to chance. My efforts paid off when she gave me the job, working twenty hours a week around my classes.

A month later, however, Natalie turned in her notice. While those in charge started looking for her replacement, I was made point person to keep things going. For almost six months, they interviewed applicant after applicant and still could not find anyone they thought would fit the team. Meanwhile, I was in talks with a local voice studio about serving as one of their instructors. But the more I talked with the studio owner, the less I felt like this was the right step for me.

"I know this sounds crazy," I told Cliff one night as we sat on the couch together after dinner, "but I've been thinking I should apply for the news director position." Cliff was supportive but cautious. He didn't want me to be disappointed if I didn't get the job. After all, what university would hire someone as their news director who didn't yet have a degree?

Still, the more I prayed about it, the more I thought I needed to at least submit my application, and after doing so, only three days passed before they hired me. For six months, I'd auditioned without knowing it, and they'd watched me work. Now, not only was I making more money than I ever had (which was not a lot, but to a twenty-year-old it felt like an enormous amount), but I would also receive my tuition completely free and Cliff would receive an enormous discount on his. I was excited to see where God would take us because I was sure he was indeed taking us somewhere.

I spent two years in that position, and I slowly started to see the success I so desired. I achieved the university's first national news coverage on one of its professors, who was an expert on all things game shows, and I flew to D.C. to interview congressmen and senators for our alumni publication, stories that ultimately received awards. I also had the rich experience of meeting and interviewing other celebrities and public figures who were often invited to campus events. But

I wanted more. I wanted more responsibility and a bigger paycheck. And so, shortly after we saw Cliff graduate with his bachelor's degree, I applied and was hired as a corporate staff writer for a Christian publishing company in Nashville. Caleb was just a year old when we moved.

Three months after I started the job, I was given the opportunity to travel to an aircraft carrier in the middle of the Eastern Mediterranean the first week of the Iraq war to cover stories of Christian sailors aboard the ship. I remember the reactions I received from some of the ladies I worked with. "How could you leave your baby to go to a war zone?" "I could never go that far away." Their comments baffled and frustrated me. Would they say the same to the male writers in our office who traveled frequently and often left their children in the care of their spouse?

I believed strongly that God had placed this opportunity in my life for a reason, and what would I be teaching my son if I always chose comfort over calling? With my husband's blessing, I took the trip, which led to another trip later that year to Baghdad, which led to my first book and ultimately to work from home.

Caleb had gone to daycare since he was six months old, and now that he was four years old, I knew I would never have another opportunity to know what it was like to be home with him before he entered kindergarten. So I left my corporate job to serve as a freelance writer from home. But the speed I worked at didn't change from one office to the other, and while my son played under my feet, I worked the days away, writing articles, submitting book proposals, and writing books for other people. I kept up my efforts to climb the ladder of success— at least the image I had placed in my mind of what success looked like.

Yesterday, though, I was climbing a much different ladder. My step-ladder. Since I'm trying to follow Martha 31, I decided our house needs to be much cleaner than it is, and I noticed the ceiling fan in our living room was really dusty. While Cliff was upstairs working, I climbed up the two steps to wipe down the fan. But height has never been one of my best traits, and only by standing on my tiptoes could I barely reach the top of the fan with my fingertips. I was halfway through wiping down the fan blades when I lost my balance.

Bam!

Almost with no warning, I fell backward on my rear end. A sharp, stabbing pain shot up somewhere near my tailbone, and I instinctively cried out. I rolled over trying to take the pressure off and alleviate the agonizing throbbing. It helped some, but I was still hurting. As tears rolled down my face, I heard my husband come running.

"What happened!" he asked.

"I fell and I think I did something to my tailbone. Ow!"

I realized I probably looked ridiculous and sounded like a baby, but at the moment, common sense and proper behavior lost out to the bruising of my behind and my ego.

Cliff scurried toward the kitchen, then came back and plopped something cold on my posterior. A bag of ice. As he checked me over, I shook my head, now half-crying, half-giggling. The sight of me sprawled out on the living room floor with an ice pack on my backside didn't feel very Proverbs 31 Wife-ish.

I had a feeling this was going to be a lot harder than I first thought.

A Proverbs 31 Wife Isn't Selfish

Yesterday *The Love Dare* told me not to be selfish. This was convicting for me, because I'm pretty sure that my selfish ways have developed greatly over the years.

When you're first married, you want to do anything and everything for the other person. But as time goes on and you get frustrated with the little things, there's a tendency to hold back, to start thinking "what about me?" You're not as free or as unselfish with time, or maybe even love. Before you realize it, you're a lot more selfish than you maybe realize.

I love my husband. But he is often the one doing things for me and not the other way around. At least that's the way I see it, though he would probably tell you differently. But it's how I feel. I think I've rationalized it a lot, made a lot of excuses about why it is, but the fact is, I need to do more for him. Be there more for him. In ways that he needs and not ways that I think he needs. Make sense?

Yesterday was a good day, not extremely eventful. As my "Love Dare," I was supposed to buy Cliff something he would like. I had trouble with this one, mainly because I wasn't sure what he would like. He had just had a birthday, so all my ideas got used at the beginning of the month since he's very hard to buy for.

We decided to go to our favorite date place for lunch. A little Japanese steakhouse that serves sushi. We always get the same thing: lo mein with vegetables, a fire crunch roll, and an Asuka roll.

The Asuka roll is manna that melts in your mouth. I (usually) save it for the end of my meal so I can savor each one. Warm tuna with avocado wrapped in seaweed and rice and set off with just a dab of spicy mayo. The roll comes in six pieces, and Cliff and I always split it, three and three. I ate my first two and then contemplated the third. Cliff had already finished his.

"Here, you can have it," I said, motioning with my chopsticks at my last bit of heaven.

Cliff looked at me, an eyebrow pointed up. "No, it's yours," he said, not moving.

"Yes, but you can have it if you want it."

"No, I don't want it. I'm good."

"Take it. I don't want to be selfish," I said.

"You're not being selfish. We each have three."

OK, maybe he had a point. So I ate my Asuka roll and tried to figure out another way I could not be selfish. (And the roll was really good.)

One of the things I've tried to do this week is not complain when he hasn't done what I've asked. Yesterday after he took Caleb to school, I moved the television upstairs to the office, next to the attic door. This is a spare, rather large and bulky TV I had moved out of the guest room when I started painting it while Cliff was gone one weekend for his Navy Reserve drill, and it has sat in the corner of our living room floor ever since. I've asked my big strong husband to move it at least five times.

So yesterday I moved it. It was heavy but moveable, and I was able to make it without too much trouble. And so far, as tempting as it has been to point it out, I haven't said anything. And he hasn't noticed. And most likely he won't. And I'm just going to let it go. That's being unselfish, right? Maybe?

I wonder how the Proverbs 31 wife, my old friend Martha 31, handled getting her husband to help with things. Or did she? I mean, did she have to ask him to take out the trash? Or move a piece of electronic equipment? Or did she just do it herself? And why is that? Why is it that it seems the wife has to do everything and the man, well, just doesn't?

I think I may have part of that answer in today's Love Dare. But it will have to wait until tomorrow.

* * *

This past weekend I attended the Beth Moore simulcast Friday night and Saturday. And even though I was busy with that, I didn't forget about the Love Dare. My assignment was to find ways to be thoughtful and avoid being rude.

The entry for Day 4 in *The Love Dare* made a statement that got me thinking about this whole relationship between a husband and wife. The chapter talks about one of the biggest differences that most of us already know when it comes to the battle of the sexes: the man tends to focus on only one thing, and the woman can multitask with the best of them. As a result, the man can often overlook things; the woman seems to be able to handle (and wants to handle) a whole lot more.

But then *The Love Dare* made a point that made me pause:

> Both of these tendencies are examples of how God designed women to complete their men. As God said at creation, "It is not good for the man to be alone; I will make him a helper suitable for him" (Genesis 2:18).

Hmmm. At first I didn't like the sound of that statement, "women to complete their men." As if the woman is merely an afterthought, an extension of another (better) sex, the male. But was I just letting feminist philosophy that permeates so much of our culture seep into my thoughts? I mean, if it is God's plan for women to complete men, then why do I fight it so much of the time? Isn't there a bigger purpose for me as a woman than just to complete my husband? What about those women who aren't married? Who do they complete? And if they don't have anyone to complete, then does that mean they have no purpose?

I can't help but think that's not God's intention.

So I started rolling over this idea of "completeness" in my mind. After all, that phrase wasn't part of the Scripture; it was from the authors of *The Love Dare*, who happen to both be men. But I'll ignore that for right now and pose a hypothesis: If a woman completes a man, then, in turn, doesn't a man complete a woman? Doesn't each sex offer the other something he or she doesn't have?

I think about my husband and all the things he is that I am not. He is a whole lot more patient than I am. A whole lot more giving. A whole lot more outwardly loving. I can be all of those things, but I have to really work at it and be intentional with it. For him, it seems to come naturally.

But on the other hand, I'm pretty assertive. I have good discernment when it comes to people and situations, and I can see things that are going to happen where Cliff has no idea. Call it a woman's intuition, but many times I've heard little warning bells go off in my head about things. Unfortunately, Cliff doesn't always listen to those. But I hope, after enough times of problems or missed opportunities because those feelings of mine have been ignored, eventually he will.

Maybe there is something more to this Love Dare. Maybe marriage itself is just one big Love Dare, one big challenge or opportunity to love someone better than I love myself, a chance for me to get just a taste of what it is for God to love the whole world, so much that he allowed his Son to die for us.

Yesterday at church my pastor continued his family series, this time speaking on parenting. It was good. In our Sunday school class afterward, the teacher mentioned that it's easy for him to relate his experience as a parent with his relationship with God as his Father in heaven. A lot of examples definitely crop up with our children that remind us of the love God has for us.

But maybe marriage is supposed to be like that too—a subtle (or sometimes not so subtle) reminder of God's love for us.

I should mention one more thing. While I was at the Beth Moore event, she spoke from Psalm 37 and mentioned that David wrote the psalm as an acrostic poem; in other words, he started each verse with the successive letters of the Hebrew alphabet. I started feeling only slightly convicted about my irreverent comments earlier about the Hebrew acrostic in Proverbs 31. It might not necessarily have been written during a drinking game.

Beth said they often did that back then so it was easier for the people to learn and remember what was being taught. I wonder if the Proverbs 31 passage was taught that way to young girls as they were growing up? Still doesn't feel quite right to me.

Saturday, the last dare I left off with, was on rudeness. My dare was to ask Cliff what things I do that drive him crazy. He said "elbows on the table," that I don't let him help me at times, and that I pick at my fingers and cuticles. All true, though I think the elbows thing isn't as big a deal as he's making it out to be (this has become some new obsession for him with both me and our son). And as far as him helping me, he's going to be leaving soon to do some Navy training, and I know from past experience I need to be less dependent on him. And the cuticle thing is simply from stress. But I can work on all of that if it will make me a better wife.

I did notice he never asked me what three things he does that drive me crazy.

a few tough
me the "
N
"

Campfires, Marshmallows, and Really Small Tents

So I've put *The Love Dare* on hold for a while since Cliff is attending a three-month Navy school in California this fall, which wraps up right before Christmas. The training he's getting is helpful, of course, but right now the regular paycheck for our family means more. It's been almost eighteen months since he returned from his first deployment—he was in Iraq for almost a year—so three months of him being away feels pretty minor to me, especially since I know we'll be able to talk to him daily. The challenge will be to figure out ways to show him love from a distance and support him as much as I can while he's away. And part of that means staying calm and not freaking out when something goes wrong and he's not here to help deal with it.

God has a great sense of humor, though, because just one week after Cliff leaves, Caleb's Cub Scout troop is scheduled for a campout. As in, let's put up tents, sleep outside, and not shower for two days and call it fun. I've never put up a tent by myself. I've never been to a Cub Scout camp. But I'm determined Caleb won't miss any of the fun his friends will have, and so when the signup list was passed around, I made a commitment we would go. Then I got on Facebook and soon wondered what I was getting myself into.

"So I've decided to go camping with Caleb and his Cub Scout troop," I posted, looking for some encouragement. After all, I know more than

, independent military wives who I was sure would give
ou'll be fine, there's nothing to it" pep talk I was looking for.
t exactly.

I *refuse* to go on campouts with my boys, that's where I draw the
ne," said one mom I knew. Even my neighbor Sharon, whose son AJ is
in the same troop as Caleb, had a good chuckle at my expense. "I pack
the snacks and wave as they leave," she wrote. "There's no way you'll see
me out there! I like my bed here at the house just fine."

"What have I gotten myself into, Mom?" I moaned to my mother
on the phone. "I don't want to disappoint Caleb, but I really *don't* want
to go camping!"

I'm pretty sure Martha 31 never slept in a tent. At least not one she
had to construct herself. Surely the men took care of that, at least. But
I'm also sure she didn't whine and complain when faced with a difficult
challenge, even one as silly as going on a campout. So I'm determined
to put my most positive face forward. We will have a great time. I think.

Cliff did manage to pull out a few things from the attic for me
that we'll need for the camping trip before he left. The tent, a battery-
powered lantern, sleeping bags, and the most important item and my
only personal request—an air mattress. And this isn't one of those flimsy,
swimming-pool kinds of mattresses; this is a queen-size mattress that
I could sleep on anywhere, even on the ground. It sure looked awfully
big, though. Cliff assured me it would fit just fine in our tent, a tent we
hadn't used in my recent memory but one he was certain fit six or seven
people. Caleb and I were good to go. We were actually doing this.

The day of the camping trip arrived sooner than I was ready for it,
but I did my best to put on my best game face—at least my best mom
face. Seeing Caleb's excitement reminded me I was doing this for him,
and it had nothing to do with whether I enjoyed it or not. I would
like it because my son liked it. So arming myself with Proverbs 31:25
("She is clothed with strength and dignity; she can laugh at the days to
come"), I dropped Caleb off at school and came home to finish getting
us packed and ready to leave that afternoon.

When Cliff left, he took with him the two soft-sided travel bags we
had, and so I decided, without giving it a whole lot of thought, to go

with our red medium-sized suitcase. We could both put our clothes in it just fine. Figuring out what to pack was a little trickier. I knew I could leave the hair dryer at home, but clothing was a little more challenging. Nashville temperatures were still warm during the day, even if it was the beginning of October, but evenings were getting colder. So I over packed. Summer shorts and T-shirts plus jeans and sweatshirts. With the amount of clothing I was bringing, I'm pretty sure we could have stayed gone for a week and been just fine.

I loaded up the car with our survival gear, including a cooler with snacks and bottled water. After checking Caleb out of school just a little early, we drove over to the parking lot where we were meeting the rest of the troop and their families and caravanning to the campsite, about a ninety-minute drive away. After waiting for about twenty minutes and being the only car in a row of pickup trucks, I was relieved to see another little car drive up and a mom and her son get out. Her name was Rebecca and she also had a Caleb who was a couple of years younger than my Caleb. She was a single mom, divorced for just a little over a year and determined that her son would get to hang out with other boys and have men around him who could be good mentors. She also wasn't that excited about the camping prospect, but like me, she was making the best of it.

Once the troop leader arrived, things moved pretty quickly. Scoutmaster Mark was from New York, a Yankee transplant to Nashville, and he did nothing to hide it. He ran a local clothing business in town, which was rumored to be struggling and causing some to wonder how long he'd be able to continue leading the troop. His attitude was usually gruff and to the point, and his less-than-gentle way of saying things, especially to parents, sometimes rubbed me the wrong way. OK, it usually rubbed me the wrong way. He cared about the kids though, which was evident in the time he took preparing for the meetings and planning activities. Still, he intimidated me, and I was already worried I was going to be the idiot parent at this campout.

It didn't take long for my fears to be proven right. After we arrived at the campsite, which belonged to the regional Boy Scout Council, everyone quickly got to work setting up tents and the camp itself since the sun was already setting. I couldn't help notice all the dads with their sons. I also couldn't help notice that I was the only one who brought a bright red suitcase to a campout. Doing my best to shrug off my insecurities, Caleb and I found a spot in a slowly forming circle of tents. I noticed our neighbor Ben, my friend Sharon's husband, and their son AJ setting up right behind us. Another reason not to look like an idiot.

Caleb and I worked at figuring out how to set up the tent using the printed instructions that miraculously were still with it. It took some extra time to figure out how to get the rain cover over it, but thanks to the help of another dad, part of the couple from India whose son was a year younger than Caleb, we were able to get it on.

But there was already a problem. This tent did not look like a six-man tent. This tent barely looked like a two-person tent. I started breathing faster as I stood there, wondering what my next step should be and not liking at all what my eyes were telling me. This tent was tiny. This tent was not going to fit a queen-size mattress. I suddenly had a visual of what it really meant to sleep out under the stars. And I didn't like it. Nor did I want to do it. But against my better judgment, I decided to do what any loyal wife who respects her husband would do (though I suspect Martha 31 would not have done this). Blow the mattress up anyway. *After all*, I thought, *if I want Cliff to have "full confidence" in me (v. 11), shouldn't I have full confidence in him? I mean, if he said this queen-size mattress would fit in this tent, this really-looks-tiny tent, then who am I to think it won't? I can't be right all the time...right?*

Caleb and I rolled out the mattress inside the tent, and I hooked up our battery-powered air pump and turned it on. As the mattress slowly filled with air, the space in the tent quickly shrank. And not just in width but height. Since the mattress was at least a good foot thick, I was pretty sure I could touch the top of the tent just rolling over.

"Uh, Mom? Where are we going to put all our stuff?"

Caleb's question was the same one I was wondering. My husband had been right. The mattress fit. But there wasn't one inch of space for anything else. Especially the unforgiving hard-sided red suitcase I'd packed all our stuff in.

OK, I thought, *we can take the mattress out and sleep on the ground, or we can maybe sleep in the car, or we could get in the car right now and just keep going...*

Ben interrupted my escape plan. "Looks like your mattress is a little big," he said, a slight smile on his face. Bless him for not actually bursting out in fits of laughter.

"Yeah, Cliff thought we had a six-man tent," I said, my eyes starting to water.

I could feel the heat rising to my face and forced myself to focus on the first thing in front of me—that stupid tent with the enormous mattress. Imagine me crying at a Cub Scout campout. My kid would never hear the end of it. I choked back the tears and cleared my throat. I was careful what I said next since I didn't want to say anything that would bring harm to my husband.

"I think we can be sure now that we don't."

"Well, I've got a six-man tent," Ben said, pointing to his site behind ours, which indeed was a big tent, complete with a separate porch-like section where you could store things. It was like a mansion compared to what I had in front of me. "AJ and I brought smaller mattresses. We can trade you those two for your big one and hopefully that will help, and you can keep your suitcase and anything else you want in our front section."

As I quickly climbed onto Mount Mattress to deflate it and make the trade, all I could do was breathe a silent prayer of thanks to God for neighbor Ben.

* * *

We made it through the campout in one piece, and despite the rough start, Caleb and I both had fun. We both got to help with kitchen duty one night making hot packets—squared-off foil packets filled with chicken and veggies, wrapped up and cooked on the fire. We enjoyed the great outdoors, and Caleb had fun with his friends going through a few different stations, earning badges in the process. I'm pretty sure, though, he had a lot more fun than I did. Still, as we drove home that Sunday morning, I felt a deep sense of satisfaction that I'd done something good. Sure it meant stepping out of my comfort zone and putting myself into situations where I had no idea what I was doing, but I'd done it all out of love for my son. (It was definitely not for love of camping.)

"I'm proud of you," Cliff told me when I got on the phone with him later that night. "I know that wasn't something you really wanted to do, but I know Caleb had a great time. And, uh, I'm sorry about the tent, but I'm glad it all worked out."

"I am too," I said sleepily as I curled up in bed on my pillow, the phone scrunched up next to my face. "But honey, just for the record?"

"Yeah, what's that?"

"The next camping trip is all you."

Getting Organized

After recovering from camping, I'm adjusting to Cliff being gone and figuring out how exactly I can still be the godly wife when my husband isn't actually here with me. (I was going to say the perfect wife, because if you read Proverbs 31 just once, you might think Martha 31 is perfect, but I'm trying to focus on her more spiritual qualities first over all of her domestic diva accomplishments.)

I have struggled with Cliff's absences in the past, particularly with his last deployment a couple of years ago. But it's a little different this time. Cliff is gone for only three months this time, not ten, and he's in California, not Iraq. And though there's still a time difference of two hours, it's not as bad as the nine we dealt with when he was serving in the Middle East. And he's not getting mortars fired at him. That right there is cause for no complaining. Ever. And given our unemployment situation right now, I'm grateful he has a way to make a paycheck.

It seems to me that Martha 31 has to be the most organized woman on the planet. She makes things, she sets and fixes the week's menu, she has a vineyard and runs what looks like multiple businesses. Chief bottle washer she is not. More like chief executive officer of much, much more.

So I've decided I need to get better organized, and I'll start with our pantry. Our pantry and I have a love-hate relationship. It starts out nice and neat, but it's determined to get as messy as possible. It gradually hides what we have, so I come home with more cream of chicken soup than we really need or those small cans of diced green chilies that we're now good to go on for three months. It'll be that long before we'll have to buy more for the rare occasion I actually cook a dish that requires them (chicken enchiladas or creamy corn chowder are usually the dishes that do it).

What makes the pantry debacle even more embarrassing is that it's always the first place my mother-in-law goes to when she comes for a visit. And it's not because she's looking for a snack. She likes to organize. She's the reason we have white wire shelves on the inside of the pantry door, because on one of her trips to our home, she went and bought them and had my father-in-law install them before they left. So now, before she's really even put down her purse, she's at my pantry, organizing boxes of instant potato mix and moving cans around so vegetables are with each other and soups sit in their own little corner.

I know a lot of women would find this annoying and some even offensive and insulting, but I don't. I guess I'm used to it, and I've learned it's her way of showing love. And because she can't sit still. Ever. She's like the Energizer Bunny with blond hair. And when it comes to cleaning and cooking, on a scale of Martha abilities, she definitely comes close to a ten. And I am quite OK with that. Especially when she organizes my pantry.

My mother-in-law, Nancy Horn, is the warmest, most welcoming person I've ever known. That was my first impression of her the night her son invited me over to their house where a bunch of his and his brother's friends from church were gathering to watch a movie. I quickly found out that was a frequent occurrence at the Horn home. Being the polite Southern girl I was brought up to be, I called her Ms. Nancy, and to this day, that's what I still call her. Since I met her when I was just nineteen, old habits die hard, and Mom or Mrs. Horn or even Nancy just never worked for me. She's always been Ms. Nancy to me.

Ms. Nancy is the type of woman who always had extra snacks and drinks in the house for all the kids who came over when her kids were still living at home. Even if she didn't drink Diet Coke, she had it in the house for Danny, one of her boys' friends. She doesn't think twice about giving something of hers away if someone else can use it, and though she denies being able to cook anything, some of the best meals I've ever had have been at her table—something she's "just thrown together."

But I know I can't wait until the next time Ms. Nancy comes for a visit for my pantry to be organized, so today I set out to make it ultimately organized. I start by pulling everything out. It spills across my kitchen counters and tables like a yard sale for food goods, and I start sorting. There are the seasonings I've had since 2005 that I'm pretty sure are tasteless by now, and the Karo syrup that's so old it's turned such a very odd grayish color that I'm not even going to try to guess if it's still good or not. There's the pickled asparagus I got in my head one day we should try, but after bringing it home, the look Cliff gave me when I showed it to him promptly canceled that idea. I throw out a whole-grain cereal with no sugar I bought at least a year ago when I was on one of my health kicks; we had one bowl of it and never touched it again. I sort and toss until finally I have everything grouped and ready to be put back in. But not yet.

I'm going to do what I've wanted to do for years. I hear plastic containers calling my name.

* * *

Well, it took a couple of hours, but after a quick trip down the street to my favorite big-box retail store (the one with the big bull's-eye for a logo), the pantry is now completely organized with beautiful, shiny clear containers of all sizes. I have containers for all of my baking ingredients like flour and sugar, slender cylindrical-shaped vessels for cereal and rice, and even a nice large one for snacks for school. I feel immensely satisfied with my work. There is something about having everything in its place.

I wonder if Martha 31 felt this when it says, "She watches over the affairs of her household and does not eat the bread of idleness" (v. 27). Because I know when the pantry gets out of sorts, it's because I'm out of sorts. Not paying attention. Not taking the time to watch out for the little things and not just the big things. That I'm more inclined to sit on my couch and watch a sappy Lifetime movie than take care of my home, and with it, my family.

I think that's what it means when Martha 31 is described as having "strength and dignity" as her clothing—what she wears, what she carries with her each day. If I carry strength each day, then I will meet each task with confidence. If I carry dignity each day, then I will meet each task with commitment.

Am I committed to being a wife and mother? Or is it something that comes and goes, like the disrepair of my pantry? And what measures that? How organized my pantry is? Or is it, as I suspect, something much more?

Sometimes the Mice
Show Up Anyway

So far, the time Cliff has been gone for this training school has been okay. Caleb is enjoying third grade, and I'm staying busy with my ministry for military wives and my writing. It helps, too, that Cliff is staying in a hotel that has Wi-Fi and we can Skype almost every night.

But of course we couldn't have him gone without at least something going wrong, and I discovered that something, or more accurately those someones, yesterday as I was working at the kitchen table on my laptop. The house was quiet, and I was in deep thought when I saw it. Something dark and furry flashed across the kitchen floor between the refrigerator and the pantry. At first I thought it was just my imagination. My eyes were playing tricks on me.

But then I happened to turn my head at the exact right moment and saw not one but *two* furry little brown rodents running in circles across my kitchen floor.

I screamed as my feet found their way to the top of the table in an instant. And I kept screaming as I watched those fuzzy mice run into each other trying to get out of sight. What nerve! What gall! It was the middle of the day! What were these mice thinking? And then two thoughts hit me: One, I'd had the same sensation of seeing a shadow pass across the floor just last week; and two, that my housekeeping apparently was so bad that even the mice were scoffing at me.

Actually, that last one wasn't the case. After calling Rachel, my neighbor, in a panic to ask what I should do, she assured me that having mice in my house had absolutely nothing to do with my personal state of cleanliness. The new school being built down the street was sending all the field mice scurrying for the hills, or in our case, into our homes. Rachel had seen three in her kitchen in just the past couple of days.

"Make sure everything in your pantry is closed up and go get some traps," she told me. I grabbed my keys and headed to the home improvement store.

"So you've got mice, huh?" the Lowes guy said, motioning me to follow him. "Yeah, that happened to me a few years ago when we had some new construction going on down the street from us. I'll show you exactly what I did that seemed to work pretty well."

Lowes Guy didn't disappoint me. And honestly, he could have shown me anything and I probably would have bought it. I was desperate. The idea of those little critters running around my house, especially while I slept, freaked me out. Lowes Guy loaded me up. He showed me mice poison for the garage and the attic and these radio frequency devices that look like little nightlights you plug into your sockets that he swears kept the mice away from his house for three years. I'm putting those in the garage and the kitchen. And finally, self-contained mousetraps that ensure I don't have to touch or see one once it's gone to its final mouse hole in the sky. I bought like four of those.

Once I'm home, I dispatch with the mouse paraphernalia quickly. Poison in the attic and garage, radio-wave thingies in the garage and in the kitchen, and one trap in the space between the cabinet and the fridge and one in the pantry. I decide to go with a little dab of peanut butter for the bait. I am a mouse slayer on a mission. And though I wish Cliff were here to deal with it all, I will not let these little rodents get the best of me! I may not yet know how to sew, but I'm going to catch me some mice! (I'm sure Martha 31 would be proud.)

It turns out I don't have to wait long. The next morning I eagerly walk into the kitchen to check on my nice-and-neat, self-contained rodent catchers, the traps I am so proud of buying because they assured that I won't have to get anywhere near a dead mouse.

"Ewwwwwww! Eeewwwwwww!"

There, to my horror, right beside the trap is the mouse. A dead, stiff-as-a-board mouse. Who can't even give me the courtesy of dying inside the trap. No, he has to have a coronary outside the trap. And now I'm stuck with the awful realization that I have to dispose of this mouse myself.

"Yuck! Gross!"

I'm squealing like a wounded animal, and I feel bad when I realize I've wakened Caleb. He rubs the sleep from his eyes as he wanders into the kitchen from his room. "Stand back!" I warn him, pointing to the dead mouse.

"Is that a dead mouse?" he asks, bending down to get a closer look.

"Yes! Now don't get too close!" I run around in a panic, my crazed motions ironically mimicking the mice I saw just yesterday running around my floor. I need a broom. A really *long* broom. One that will reach across the room. From the opposite end. I head to the laundry room and grab the only broom we have and the handy dustbin that has a lid that closes. But first I need to put on shoes. Because there's no way I'm going to try to sweep that dead rodent away and have it touch my toes. A shiver, and not the first one, runs through me.

After I finally stop squealing, I try to focus on what's next. Removing the dead mouse. I'm also trying to ignore Caleb, who is finding all of this very entertaining. "Mom, what if the mouse isn't really dead? What if he's just faking, and he's gonna trick you?"

I know he's messing with me, but I stop and take a look at my beaming, grinning son. "Out." I say, pointing to his room. He chuckles, quite amused and pleased with himself, and runs off.

I quickly sweep the stiff mouse into the dustbin, close it up, and march it across the living room into the garage and over to the garbage can and into a waiting garbage bag I've put there. There's only one problem. When I turn the dustbin over and tap it, I see no mouse in the bag. I look again. I look around the garbage can. I look on the garage floor. Nothing.

The mouse is still in the house.

I suddenly have this vision of a dead mouse lying across my couch, and I quickly double back to find him. I can't find him anywhere. I've taken up my crazy rodent-like running patterns again, and Caleb has emerged for a second time to giggle at his crazy mother. Finally, I go back to look in the garage one more time. There he is. He fell behind the garbage can. I get the broom, sweep him up yet again in the dustbin, and this time make sure he makes it into the garbage bag.

I was really hoping his death would be a warning to all the others and they would just leave immediately. Unfortunately, I ended up catching two more—this time both in the traps—and while I'm glad I didn't have to touch them, it still isn't exactly appealing to look for grey fur and whiskers to confirm the trap has indeed caught one.

But as unappealing as the whole mouse-catching business is, I'm not about to keep it from Cliff. I want him to know every crazy detail. I want him to know he's married to a mouse slayer.

I want him to know I am more than ready for him to come home.

Running the Race

A couple of years ago Cliff and I started running 5Ks together. Just writing that makes me feel so athletic. But it's so not even remotely the truth. I would not say that either of us are real runners. We do it mostly for the exercise, and we're not consistent by any stretch of the imagination. Still, it's been something that we've enjoyed doing when we can do it together. As much as it makes us want to throw up afterward.

The town where we live is holding its first Grey Ghost 5K. Adults run the 5K, kids run a mile. But this year, Cliff's in California and I've enlisted Caleb to take his place. My in-laws also decided to come up the same weekend as the run, which is also the weekend of Halloween.

"There's nothing in here I can organize!" I hear Ms. Nancy exclaim as she stands in the corner of our kitchen looking into our pantry. Caleb has started calling it the astronaut closet because all the clear plastic containers look very futuristic and almost out-of-this-world to him. You know you haven't done the best job at housekeeping when your kid thinks a well-organized pantry must mean you have a time machine hidden somewhere.

"Sorry!" I say, though secretly I'm not. Mission accomplished. I'm hoping by the time Ms. Nancy is in her eighties I'll actually have a house that's clean and well-organized. So far the jury's out on whether that will ever happen.

I'm in the living room finishing up my costume for Halloween. I am not a fan of this holiday. I grew up in a family that didn't trick or treat, and if we did dress up, it was as Bible characters for a fall festival at our church. As we got older, I think my parents eventually relented, or wore down, and we did get to walk around the block a couple of times, begging with the rest of the kids for candy bars and Tootsie Rolls. But Halloween has never been my favorite holiday. I don't like scary, and I don't really care about dressing up. My husband, on the other hand, loves the holiday. His family trick or treated with gusto, and their costumes were always creative and fun. So when Caleb came along, Cliff and I compromised. Caleb could dress up and go trick or treating, but scary was out of the question.

We've never had a problem with that basic rule until this year. While the three of us were out one day, Caleb found a werewolf costume in a store and begged to get it. If there was ever a "friendly" version of a werewolf, it was this one, and so after a huddle with Cliff, we relented and let Caleb get it. I thought, *At least Halloween is taken care of.*

Turns out I was wrong. Last week Caleb announced he didn't want to go as a werewolf for Halloween. He wanted to go as a TV, his "favorite thing!" While I'm all about being creative, it didn't exactly warm my heart. Who wants their child to dress up as something so many people know as the boob tube? But Caleb was already dreaming up the design for his costume and had this elaborate plan for how he would act out his favorite shows. And then he had another idea.

"Mom, what are you going to go as?" he asked, as I was cutting out a big brown box I had grabbed from the attic that would be his television.

"I have the perfect costume in mind," I said absentmindedly, eyeballing his body as I started to figure out the width of the box and how much I was cutting and how I was exactly doing it. "How about I go as Caleb's mom?"

"Mooooommmm!" I got the look. "That's not a costume."

"Why can't it be a costume?" I asked.

I decided instead of putting a hole in the top of the box and risking his neck getting rubbed raw, we'd take a side-of-the-box approach and cut out the back in a round shape with holes in the side that he could put his arms through.

"Because, you're my mom every day. You need to be something else for Halloween."

"OK, what do you think I should be?"

"A remote!"

So that is why I'm now kneeling on the floor in my living room cutting out black material to make my "remote" costume. I've decided there's no way I'm going to fit myself in a box version, so we're going with the softer version—black sheets I found on sale at the store, holes in the sides for the arms, glued around the edges except for a hole in the neck and at the bottom. Grey foamboard that I'm using to cut out all the buttons, which will be glued on with some sticky fabric glue I bought. I can hear the "push your button" jokes already starting.

* * *

October 31 started early for us this year. My mom, who lives just down the street, and Ms. Nancy were both nice enough to come with us to the 5K and the mile Caleb and I ran this morning. Caleb ran first, and then while I ran, they kept an eye on him.

Caleb did a great job. Nowhere near first, but he finished, and that's the goal for both of us. To finish.

Then it was my turn. The throng of runners slowly started making their way onto the countryside course, and after I found my pace and my breathing settled into a rhythm, my mind had time to turn elsewhere. I thought about this personal race I'm starting. Though it's not really a race, I suppose, because I don't ever want to stop being a good wife and mom. I just want to keep going.

But it's definitely a marathon. Like the course I ran today, being a wife and mom comes with flat and easy, steep and exhausting, bumps in the road and smooth going at other times. The views can be great, beautiful, daunting, and did I mention exhausting? I think about Cliff being away from us right now and the uncertainties we still face. Unemployment, or underemployment as the new term goes these days, sucks. It is not for the faint of heart. And as the spouse of someone without full-time work, it's difficult to know what to do. How far to push. How much to encourage. How accepting to be. How worried to act. How much understanding to show.

I've run out of ideas.

Just this week, Cliff had interviews by phone for a radio station with two positions open at two of its stations in Arizona and California. But they need the new hires to start next month, in November. Cliff, however, is in training until December. And the Navy is not exactly the type of employer that allows you to leave to check out other opportunities. There's no time off for good behavior. There's no boss you can expect to be understanding and let you do what you need to do "just this once." And though Cliff thought the interviews went well, he knew he was limited in what he could do as an applicant. He got the call yesterday letting him know he would not be considered any further for those jobs. Disappointed? Yes. Surprised? I guess not.

We agreed for him to take this military training because it was good for his Navy career and good for our family in that it meant three months of steady income even if it meant three months apart. But I wasn't expecting this opportunity to get in the way of other opportunities.

But we keep running. Even when we're out of breath, as I was on the course today, and even when we just want to stop. We keep running. We keep going. And the most important part, I think? We keep running together. And just as I finished the 5K today with a pretty decent time of 34:20, we hope to finish this race of ours well.

Pretty sure Martha 31 would agree.

Extreme Cake Baking

I think I have found my thing in Caleb's Cub Scout troop. Well, technically, it's not supposed to be my thing. Technically, it's supposed to be a father and son doing this next project, but since Cliff is away, Caleb's got me. And it's going to be good. I hope.

Scoutmaster Mark announced last night that for November's den meeting, we're baking cakes. But not just any kind of cake. Extreme cakes. Like the kind of cakes we're always watching people make on food channels. The only rule is everything on the cake has to be edible.

So after school today Caleb and I sat down to plan our strategy. I could feel the temptation building. The tingling enticement to a parent who really wants to win, a feeling so powerful it lures you in until you've designed the science project or written the paper or created the cake yourself, and your kid is sitting off to the side wondering when his project became yours. But as much as I would love for us to win, I also want this to be fun for Caleb. So I'm resisting the urge to do it all and instead, letting Caleb plan it out. Though I do reserve the right to offer suggestions where I think they may help. That's just what a good parent does, right?

I didn't have to offer many. It turns out my son may share some of my competitiveness. After enjoying his time at the campout, Caleb decided he wants to recreate it. We sketched out a long rectangle cake with a round cake on top that will depict a hill where Cub World is. Cub World was a special section of the camp that the Cub Scouts loved. We'll use ice-cream cones for trees and fruit rollups and pretzels to make a couple of tents. We'll also be sure to have a standard-issue red bucket of water by the camp fire for emergencies—but I'll leave the red suitcase out this time.

* * *

This Saturday we took a drive over to my favorite craft store to find all the supplies we'll need to make the cake. Part of what I'm trying to figure out in this quest to be Martha 31 is how to do so much without spending so much too. But as we were walking up and down the cake-decorating aisles, I quickly saw that cake decorating is expensive, and I'm not so sure how Cliff will feel about my purchases. After seeing the price of fondant, I quickly ruled that out as an option. Ace of Cakes this will not be. Buttercream it is. Though we did buy a little kit of fondant to use to make letters. And we found some brown modeling chocolate that Caleb decided would be great to use to make a bear. Granted, we saw no bears while we were camping, but our cake will have a bear. I also bought a huge sheet-cake pan and two round pans along with a frosting spatula. The rest of the supplies we bought at the grocery store on the way home. Pretzels, two different sizes. Ice-cream cones. Fruit rollups. And Whoppers Milk Chocolate Malted Milk Balls.

I knew there was no way we could create this cake in one night. So my plan was to decorate the trees the first night. Bake the cake the second night. And decorate the entire thing the third night, just in time to bring the finished product to the monthly Cub Scout meeting the next night. Though I'm not entirely sure I would want to eat the cake at that point...

But that's what we did. And Caleb helped with all of it. I admit there were a couple of times that I *really* had to resist the urge to do it all myself. He had fun decorating the trees with uneven wavy lines. Though the next night's actual baking got a little boring for him until I let him lick the mixing beaters. (Yes, I know, kids shouldn't eat cake batter just like they should never ride a bike without a helmet or cross the street without a parent holding their hand. I can't believe I'm still alive.) He also had fun spreading the bright green buttercream frosting all over.

The next night was the night to decorate the whole thing. This was the moment. It was do or die. Our plan was either going to work or not.

Part of our original idea was to create a sign made out of a graham cracker that said, "Don't feed the bears." But that proved a lot harder than we realized. Our frosting wasn't thick or strong enough to bond the graham cracker with the pretzel sticks serving as posts to hold up the sign. And though I read up on royal icing, this was supposed to be a completely edible cake, and I wasn't sure if royal icing would get us disqualified or not. So we improvised. We did away with the bear sign and instead, Caleb used the fondant kit we'd bought to create letters that spelled out Cub World. Each letter went on a pretzel stick. Not perfect, but it worked.

And that was my goal. Really, what any well-meaning, project-helping parent's goal should be: Make it work, but don't let it look too perfect. You don't want to be blamed for helping too much, now do you? My biggest goal though was for us to have fun. For Caleb to enjoy baking a cake and using his imagination and learning to think out of the box a little bit.

* * *

Last night was the big cake competition at Caleb's troop meeting. I had no idea what our competition was going to be so I tried not to get Caleb's hopes up, but inside, I was really hoping we would win. A baker I am not. But I have to admit, I thought our cake was in the top five at least. There were round cakes with archery targets on top, a lot of sheet cakes with trees, and one cake had also done tents but used graham crackers (that would have been so much easier than those sticky fruit rollups). Caleb's cake was the only one there that had a sheet cake with a round cake on top.

I resisted rolling my eyes at the cake one of the female scout leaders brought in for her son. It was complete with frosting so perfectly piped all around the cake that it looked as close to professional as I'd seen. Pretty sure her son didn't touch that cake. I was starting to get worried.

Each cake, set out on two tables, received a number, and there were five categories that a winner would be selected in. Best-Looking Cake to Eat, Most Creative, and a few others I can't remember. Caleb was nervous but excited.

At the end of the night, the winners were announced—and Caleb's cake won Most Creative! He was so excited! But his excitement was cut short when Scoutmaster Mark announced that all the cakes would be delivered to different public services (the fire station, the police station) and churches in the community as our way of saying thank you for what they do.

Tears started streaming down my son's face. "But I wanted to eat my cake!" I tried holding back the thought that after working on that thing for three days, storing it in the refrigerator but without any container to keep it really fresh, I was pretty sure I did not want to taste that cake.

In the end, with help from his den leader, Caleb agreed it was a nice thing to bring the cake to someone else to share. But he still wasn't happy that he never got to taste it. Note to self: Next time we do an extreme cake, make a smaller cake he can eat.

What's a Wife to Do?

I've been contemplating this whole idea of the Proverbs 31 wife. Even though Cliff isn't here, I'm trying my best to be the supportive wife he needs. I try to listen patiently to how his day has gone and not be overeager to share what my day's been like, especially if it's one of those days where I'd rather complain than rejoice. He's enjoying his class and doing well on his tests. I'm proud of him for finding a church to go to near his base and making a point to go each Sunday.

For me, this time that he's been away has not been bad. I think it's because I've tried as much as possible to have a consistent quiet time and keep my focus on God and his plan for my day and for my family's day. I've stayed busy with my ministry and handling last revisions for my new book that comes out in a few months.

I started Wives of Faith right before Cliff's first deployment, with the help of an Army wife and a core group of about ten ladies that first year we did it in Nashville. It's grown to a few local groups around the country with a lot of women connecting online via our website and community group. I've moved away from writing for other people and now I'm writing my own books, and my focus right now is providing resources for the military wife. It's my passion. I love encouraging these precious ladies. Some of my best ministry takes place on Facebook when I can pray for military wives who contact me.

Praying for Cliff consistently also helps. It's hard to get uptight or fed up with someone when you're constantly taking him to God in prayer. (Though sometimes it's the being fed up part that causes you to pray in the first place.) Still, praying helps. It's a good reminder I am not in control.

Control may be one of the secrets to Martha 31. She seems to be in control of everything. I keep going back to the verse where she is "clothed with strength and dignity; she can laugh at the days to come" (v. 25). That is some serious control! On one hand, it tells me about her character—she's strong. She doesn't let a lot ruffle her. On the other, more thankful note, she has bad days too. (Which, if you read all the verses before this one, you could really start to wonder if she has *ever* been frustrated.)

I'm not sure I can always laugh at the days to come. Right now, those days have a lot of question marks. We're not sure what will happen after Cliff comes home. And that doesn't help me feel as if I'm in control. A lot feels as if it's *out* of my control.

I wish the Proverbs 31 wife passage had a hint of how Martha 31 handled it when she did have a bad day. Did she let the house get messy? Did she ever burn the dinner? Was she ever left with more bills than paycheck at the end of the month?

So what's a wife to do? Control what she can; give to God what she can't? But I keep looking at this laundry list of things Martha 31 does. That's a lot to control. It makes me tired just looking at it. Of course, I guess if I were to list out everything I do, I'd feel tired with that list as well. But I'm not so sure that list reflects well on me. How much of my list reflects care for my family?

For years, I've made "making a difference" my priority. And sometimes, if I'm painfully honest, that difference would be for my career. My desires. My wants. My hopes and dreams. From as early as I can remember, I loved to make a difference for other people. Loved doing mission projects at church when I was a kid. In high school, I started a local chapter of Students Against Driving Drunk (now known today as Students Against Destructive Decisions). And after writing a story for my school paper on English as a Second Language students, I started a tutoring group that brought my friends together with international students for help with homework as well as friendship. Most of the time my intention is to ultimately bring glory to God. But on my terms. Not always for the benefit of my husband. Not always for the benefit of my child.

I know other wives who are the exact opposite. Everything they do is for their families. They throw themselves into being room mom at their kids' schools and they plan elaborate parties for their husbands' jobs and they become coupon gurus and shopping mavens and their families' personal Paula Deens.

I want the middle. I don't want either extreme. I want to honor God and honor my family at the same time. I want to feel satisfied in both my work and my home. Truthfully, I'm not there. When I'm knee-deep in ministry or writing, I'm often thinking of what I'm missing with my family. And when I'm with my family, I'm thinking of what I could be doing in my ministry.

Did Martha 31 run around like the proverbial chicken? Or did she just take one day at a time? Did she do all those things she's credited with all at once? Or did they come in seasons, in spans of time, in moments of clarity and purpose? Did her actions follow the wisdom she collected over a lifetime and not just a week?

I still have a whole lot more questions than answers.

What Do I Make?

I miss you."

This phrase always becomes our nightly greeting and good-bye when Cliff's away. My husband is my best friend. We enjoy doing everything together. We enjoy being together. I know couples who hardly do anything in the same room, but Cliff and I aren't that way. And with Thanksgiving not too far off, the thought of being apart is not an appealing one in the slightest.

Right now I'm planning to spend it here at home with Caleb and my mom. Cliff is thinking of driving north to the San Francisco area where his aunt and uncle live. But I'm very tempted to fly out there to see him. The thought of spending money on plane tickets when we could save that money leaves me torn, though.

We talked about it over Skype. After Thanksgiving, Cliff will have three more weeks for the class he's taking for the Navy. It's been a long, hard, demanding class, and I can tell he's tired and ready for a break. Flying out there may be just the motivation he needs to finish strong. And isn't it my job to "bring him good, not harm" (v. 12)?

I've looked at tickets. Prices aren't too bad right now, though I imagine they'll get higher the longer we wait.

I decide we're going. It will be a nice visit with Cliff, and we'll get to see family we don't always have the opportunity to hang out with. And Aunt Becky and Uncle Hal and their clan are a lot of fun to be around.

* * *

"Hello!"

Aunt Becky, a Queen by marriage, greeted us with a big smile and a hug as we met her coming out of the airport. In her early sixties with short blond hair, she's three years older than her sister, Ms. Nancy, but still looks much younger than her actual age.

When Cliff and his brother and sister were kids, they'd get together for a couple of weeks during the summer with Aunt Becky's kids at their grandmother's in the little Mississippi town where their parents grew up. Though everyone's now grown with kids of their own, they still talk fondly of those summer days.

This was the first time our little family of three had been out to their house on the West Coast. The Queens moved out there from Louisiana a few years ago to help take care of Uncle Hal's mom, who passed away last year. Aunt Becky, who once went to college on a women's basketball scholarship, now spends her days playing with her grandchildren, baking, sewing, and keeping up with family and friends on Facebook and by phone. She's one of the most thoughtful people I've ever met, and despite some health challenges, she always seems to be doing for others.

Cliff arrived later that night, and it was a sweet reunion for sure. It was so nice just to be near him again. The rest of the week was spent visiting with Becky and Hal, their daughter Jennifer and her husband, Doug, and their two little boys, and seeing some of the sights of San Francisco as a family.

Jennifer is a stay-at-home mom and loves it. Though she's done everything from teaching school (her degree is in education) to working for a major office supply company, hosting big clients with fancy lunches and dinners, she seems extremely satisfied just being a mom. She takes care of their beautiful house while Doug works, and she's always working on a project to find the perfect piece of furniture or make the best arrangement of pictures or artwork for their walls.

What strikes me most about both Becky and Jennifer is their enjoyment in making things—Becky sews beautiful pillows, among other things, and Jennifer definitely has an eye for creating a beautiful room. She has helped Ms. Nancy decorate her entire house several times. They may not make a mark in a company or in the work world, but they certainly make a mark in their households. For their families.

It makes me beg the question, what am I making for my family? What am I investing into them? Into our home? And what are they getting out of it? I don't even think I'm talking about decorating at this moment, though I'm sure I could do a much better job than I've done. What, in fact, am I leaving behind?

Aunt Becky's home holds a lot of things that have been passed down from wife to wife over generations. There's a loving legacy that sits on those walls and inside them. My mother-in-law's home is very similar. Old black and white photos of her mother and father on their wedding day. Reading glasses from a great-great-great aunt. A family Bible that's been handed down for generations. Is it just a matter of making things beautiful? Or does it go deeper than that? Does it go to the spirit of what beauty is? Does a beautiful home ensure a beautiful spirit?

Not necessarily. But a beautiful spirit can make a beautiful home. And maybe that's what I need to work on creating.

What's Next?

After enjoying the time together through Thanksgiving, welcoming Cliff home right before Christmas, and spending quality family time the last week of the year, January has hit with a thud. It's like enjoying the party and the fun the night before and waking up the next morning realizing there's a big mess to clean up. Our mess is the realization that we have no idea where the next paycheck is coming from, and though our faith that God will provide remains strong because we've already seen him bring us this far, still the unknown is daunting and scary.

I want to be the supportive wife. The wife that is my husband's biggest cheerleader. The best encourager. The woman who knows just what to say and when to say it. But it's not always my husband's strength to listen. Whether it's what some might call plain old woman's intuition or, for me, the spiritual gift of discernment, I've always had this ability to see what's coming. Especially when it comes to jobs and jobs possibly ending. That's what I saw for Cliff after he got back from his first deployment.

"Honey, I just keep thinking you need to start looking for something else," I would tell him. The nonprofit radio station where he worked had already laid off a couple of people while he was gone, with budget cuts cited as the reason. As the marketing director, his position didn't seem that secure to me since companies often make that the first position cut in tough times. But Cliff wouldn't listen. He's an extremely loyal guy, and it was hard for him to think a boss or a company wouldn't be the same way for him. He was so eager to get back into his job and show his bosses he could do it well.

Unfortunately, he didn't really get the chance. Six months after returning from combat duty, his position was cut from the radio station. With two weeks of severance. Who knew that when he finished one war, he'd come home to start another, fighting unemployment?

And it has been a fight. He's applied with so many companies I've lost count. And each time he's been invited to interview with a company, he's made it to the second or final stage, usually with just one or two other applicants competing for the job. But he's never been given the final rose, so to speak. And experiencing rejection after rejection has been hard on him. And hard for me.

While he's heard no repeatedly, I've been told yes. With freelance jobs. New book deals. More opportunities for my ministry to military wives. Not all monetary successes, but the ball still feels as though it's rolling forward. Cliff's often feels as though it's stuck.

How do you handle that as a wife? For that matter, how do you handle that as a husband?

I've talked to other wives who have been there with their husbands. One friend told me in long detail how she helped her accountant husband, after losing one job, find another. She wrote his resume for him. She found and compiled the list of potential job openings in their area. She wrote his introductory letter, and ultimately it was she who got him his next job. She was so proud of her accomplishment she included it in the essay she had to write when she applied for an MBA program. She got accepted.

Ms. Nancy has also told me many times how she helped Cliff's dad find a job after they were forced to leave the Navy because of a medical discharge. She made the calls and did the legwork. She found him a job and their family a place to live. Am I being completely selfish thinking my husband should find his own job? Am I failing in a wife's duty?

I look at Martha 31 and nowhere in her passage does it say she found work for her husband. Surely she had plenty of work for herself. And not just around the house, but through her own businesses.

Which makes me wonder—did she do *all* the work while her husband just hung out at the city gate and checked his bank account each afternoon when he got home to see what the little missus brought in?

I want to encourage my husband, but am I encouraging him by doing everything for him? Or am I just resisting what a wife is supposed to do?

One of those quizzes going around on Facebook asks the question, "What kind of wife are you?" My result, after working through the quiz, was that I'm a "modern wife." A wife who helps her husband but expects her husband to help as well. A fifty-fifty partnership. I was feeling pretty good about it until I saw how many friends of mine also took the quiz and were rated as the "perfect wife," defined as a wife who has dinner on the table when her husband comes home and is there for whatever he needs. So which wife does God want me to be? A modern wife? Or a perfect wife?

And is there really such a thing?

How do I support my husband like Martha 31? Being able to cook a gourmet meal or sew curtains or keep a beautifully decorated house right out of the pages of a magazine doesn't seem as urgent when we're wondering if we'll be able to pay the mortgage next month.

Maybe I can be a modern version of Martha 31. Even if I'm not so perfect.

Beauty Skin Deep

'm looking forward to this coming week. For one week, Cliff and I will get away from the stress that has become our life. We're joining his parents and his sister's family for a cruise to the Bahamas. Ms. Nancy does a lot of tours and trips for a small travel agency, and this one offered a great rate. We signed up for it last year when our financial situation was a lot better, and since it's already paid for, we're going to go and enjoy it. This will be Caleb and his cousins' first cruise, and I'm just looking forward to some time away.

It also coincides with Super Bowl week, and with the ship leaving out of New Orleans and the Saints playing in the championship for the first time, it should be a very exciting cruise. Let's just hope they win.

We drove down to Cliff's parents' home just outside Baton Rouge, and the next day we piled into vehicles and caravanned to the ship's port in New Orleans. Being February, it was chilly, even for the Crescent City, but we looked forward to getting on board and showing Caleb the ship.

Cliff and I had cruised before, many years earlier, for our honeymoon. I remembered making such a big deal about formal night, the evening where everyone dresses up for dinner. I'd borrowed a dress from Cliff's sister and had my hair fixed in the ship's salon, in an upside-down French twist. I'd insisted Cliff wait out in the lounge while I slipped into my dress so he could get the full effect. He met me that night with a rose.

This week I was less concerned about dressing up than just relaxing. But I did have one thing I wanted to do. I wanted a visit to the ship spa. I knew I wouldn't be able to afford to do much, but I wanted to do at least something. With Caleb hanging out with his cousins in Nana's cabin for a while, Cliff and I walked over to the spa to view the services and prices. I settled on a special they were offering that included a mini-facial, a hair-conditioning treatment, and a pedicure. I set my appointment for the next day. I couldn't wait.

❊ ❊ ❊

Heidi met me at the receptionist desk and ushered me back to her station. She was young, not more than twenty, and she told me it had always been her dream to work on a cruise ship, a job she'd just started about four months earlier. Before that she'd worked in a salon in her hometown and had been doing hair since she was fifteen. She was blond with a thin athletic build, and her skin looked flawless.

"So, let me ask you a few questions first," she said, pulling out a tiny clipboard and a pen and sitting on a rolling stool in front of me. She first asked me what I did, and I told her I was a writer and I'd just finished up one book and was working on another. As she examined my skin under an ultraviolet light, she shook her head and did little to mask her disgust.

"How often do you wash your face?"

I cringed inside. Now we were getting personal.

"Um, well, I do wash my face, but I admit it's been kind of stressful lately and I haven't really taken much time to do it."

"Do you use a moisturizer? What about toner?"

"Moisturizer, yes. Toner, not always."

Heidi looked me up and down as she scribbled something on her sheet. "You know, I see women every day in here who don't take care of their skin, and there really is no excuse for not doing it."

I could feel my stomach knotting up. This wasn't exactly the relaxing hour I had pictured. I started wondering if I could just get up and leave.

Ms. Clear Face continued. "I mean, you should never go to bed without removing your makeup, and you should always use a cleanser and a moisturizer and I recommend a toner. See my face? I wash it every night and I never have a problem with breakouts or blackheads."

You've also never been a wife or a mom, I thought. *Talk to me after you've carried around an entire other person for nine months or slept an average of four hours at a time. Pretty sure your skin won't look the same then either.*

"Do you drink water? Do you eat a lot of fruits and vegetables?"

The inquisition seemed to last forever. All I wanted was to close my eyes and relax. Finally, she lowered my chair and started working on my face. I was a little disappointed that it would be right out in the open where everyone else was having things done. I was used to facials being done in quiet rooms with soft music and the sound of running water. I guess I knew now what "minifacial" left out. But after the lecture I'd just received, I wasn't exactly feeling peaceful anyway.

I slowly turned over what she'd just said in my mind. I wondered if Martha 31 worried about her looks. We're told she clothes herself in "fine linen and purple" (v. 22). So maybe she does take care to dress nicely. But we're also told that "beauty is fleeting" and the most important thing is a "woman who fears the LORD is to be praised" (v. 30). It doesn't say the good-looking woman or the beautiful woman.

But we've been told over and over that men recognize beauty. It's in their DNA. They respond to it. Even babies have been observed to react more favorably to people who are pretty than people who are not.

So is it part of following the footsteps of Martha 31 to pursue beauty? To be beautiful? To make a conscious effort to put on makeup and fix my hair and wear outfits that look put together rather than just thrown on? If it makes a difference for my husband, isn't it important?

On the flip side, taking time out each night to take care of my face, working out a few times a week to exercise my body—couldn't that also have an effect on my attitude, which in turn would have an effect on my family?

As annoyed as I was with Ms. Perfect Face, by the end of the appointment I made a quiet resolution to not be so fast at putting my looks after everything else.

Praying for Answers

As I continue to study the Proverbs 31 wife, my heart and my head recognize a few things. For one, the wife so many say we want to emulate and look up to may not have been an actual person. If you read the first ten verses of Proverbs 31, you realize the section about Martha 31 might be included in sayings from a King Lemuel, sayings he learned from his mother (v. 1). If that's the case, the verses about Martha 31 express the ideals a mother is holding up to her son to look for as he seeks a wife. (Counter to this, many biblical scholars I've read believe Proverbs 31:10-31 is most likely from an anonymous writer and not from King Lemuel or his mother.)

Regardless of who actually wrote these verses, "a wife of noble character" or "an excellent wife" is considered a rare find (v. 10). She's not necessarily the common woman.

I don't need to be the rare jewel (realistically, I know I probably never will be). But I would love to be the jewel in my husband's eyes. The jewel God put in Cliff's life. And despite what Cliff tells me, sweet man that he is, I know I have a long way to go.

If there's anything I know I can learn from Martha 31 right now, it's my desire to be devoted to God. Because when my heart is focused on him and his guidance, I'm a whole lot nicer to be around. I have a much stronger tendency to serve my family. So in this state of uncertainty that our family finds itself, I know my energy, my focus, needs to be less on fixing and more on focusing. On God. On his provision.

On his direction. Because if past experience has taught me, God does amazing things when we stop trying to take care of it all ourselves.

So no more nagging. No more suggested solutions. No more "if he would just do it my way." Just a whole lot of prayer. And in turn, I hope, a whole lot of love. And no matter what happens, trust that God will provide.

* * *

When Cliff was training in California, I had talked with him about moving my office downstairs. Actually, it was his suggestion. We have a large bonus room that's located over the garage, and we've always used it as an office space, not ever a play space for Caleb or an extra den or family room as other families do. It's a huge space and gives us room for our bookshelves and (mostly my) many books.

But everyone needs a change now and then, and I was at that point. So while he was away, I moved my desk (with help from Cliff's twin, Clay, who happened to be in town one weekend) into our spare guest-room and added a few nice-size dry erase boards on the walls.

With Cliff home, I think it's been an adjustment for him not to have me up there as I was before, but for me, it's been nice to have what I call "thinking space." He's staying busy on a freelance job doing radio buys for women's events for the company we both used to work for. And looking for full-time work, the never-ending assignment.

But bills also never end, and though we enjoyed the income while it lasted, what Cliff earned last fall is quickly running out. Recently I got a message from a former boss who is looking for a marketing director for the college he's dean of at a Christian university in South Carolina. It seems to be a natural fit with my skills, and while I haven't wanted to go back to a "real" job, our family has reached a point where I probably need to seriously consider it. Except when I first mentioned it to Cliff, he was less than thrilled.

"South Carolina? But that would mean leaving Nashville." Change doesn't bother me much. I enjoy changes and usually get a rush at starting something new. Getting a fresh start. My husband isn't that way.

And I could see a little fear in his eyes at the thought of all the change. But I'm not sure we have a whole lot of options.

"Hey." Cliff stood at the door of my office with a smile on his face. A record label he has always wanted to work for had just posted an open position for a marketing and promotions rep. "I've sent in my resume and I've made a couple of calls to people I know who work there," he told me.

I could tell he felt good about this and my heart started beating fast. Maybe this is what we've been waiting for. This was a dream job for Cliff—a job he's wanted since we moved to Nashville five years ago. Maybe God had this in mind for him all along.

Against my better judgment, trying to forget all the disappointments we've had, I started getting excited. And at the very least, I wanted to show excitement for Cliff. I committed right then to start fervently praying for this job.

See, I've seen God do some amazing things in my life. And I want that desperately for my husband. Cliff has walked with me through those opportunities, always with support and encouragement and never a word of "why not me?" But my prayer these days has been that God would give Cliff an amazing moment—a moment that without a doubt shows Cliff God has special plans for him. A special purpose for his life. That he's not meant to be "Sara's sidekick." My words and my prayer, not necessarily shared by my husband.

So I've started praying for Cliff. Each morning when I wake up, I make a point to pray for this job he's applied for, for the guy who's managing the applications and who will be making the decision. I'm praying for the interview we don't yet know is going to happen, that God helps Cliff say exactly what he needs to, and that God gives Cliff this job. And I can tell God is doing something in me as I'm praying.

Because here is a deep confession. I usually pray the hardest for things that have to do with me. My wants. My desires. My hopes and dreams. I pray for Cliff and Caleb and other family members from time to time, but if I'm really honest, and this book is all about honesty (there's no point in writing it if it isn't), my biggest prayers usually have to do with me. Selfish prayers. Self-absorbed prayers. The things God must think sometimes when he hears my prayers of me, myself, and I.

But these days I'm praying for Cliff. For his happiness. For his confidence. His joy and peace. For his dream. And as I do so, I think less about my goals and dreams and more about my husband's.

Though the timing couldn't be more interesting.

This past week I got an email that made me literally squeal with happiness. It was a message from a producer for Focus on the Family. They reviewed my book that just came out (*GOD Strong: A Military Wife's Spiritual Survival Guide*) and are considering doing an interview with me.

Oh. My. Goodness. To me, Focus on the Family has always been the Oprah for Christian authors. Ever since I started writing books, it's been a dream of mine to be on Focus. What a thrill that would be.

I filled out the requested forms, answered their questions, and soon received another email asking if I could do a pre-interview with them. A pre-interview, usually done by phone, is an audition or a screening to help them make a final decision on whether to invite someone onto the show. Pre-interviews can be hit and miss. It all depends on what the show is looking for.

When the producer called, I stood there in my office and answered her questions (I think and talk better standing up), sharing my thoughts about military spouses and deployment and what I've discovered about leaning on God's strength to get through it. She asked some great questions, and I really enjoyed the conversation. I tried not to get my hopes up too high, but I felt the interview went well, and I was excited to see if I might be invited to do the actual interview.

However, even as I answered her questions, my heart was focused on my husband and my prayer was this: "God, I would rather see Cliff get this job of his dreams than for me to ever go on Focus on the Family." It was as sincere a prayer as I've ever prayed, and the more I prayed it, the more desperate I became for it to happen. For me to even say those words, I knew my heart was changing, that God was doing something in my life as a wife learning to put her husband before herself. And I meant every word.

* * *

Cliff had his interview today. And I've been praying nonstop. I posted it on Facebook some twenty times, and I know others have been praying for him too. The whole time he was gone, I stayed on my knees in our living room. Asking God for his grace. Asking God for his mercy. For his kindness toward Cliff. That he would step up for Cliff. That Cliff would see this job become a reality and that he would see God's hand in it in an amazing way. Because I've seen God's hand in my life. And I so want that for my husband.

But being told no over and over hasn't made it easy for Cliff to see God's hand. No one likes to be rejected. I know Cliff isn't the only one. I know there are many other families out there struggling with the same situation. But today is Cliff's day. It has to be. After eighteen months of wondering, we are ready to stop. A little certainty for a while would be nice. It would be great.

So I've prayed. And I anxiously waited to hear what Cliff had to say about the interview.

His call came about forty minutes later than I was expecting. His interview had gone for more than an hour. That's a great sign, right? The manager asked him all the expected questions. Stuff about his experience, what his weaknesses were, what his strengths were. Cliff felt good about the interview. He was confident he would get invited back for at least another.

They'd asked about his reserve experience and the possibility of another deployment. Technically they're not supposed to, but almost every company Cliff has ever interviewed with has. His standard answer is, "There's always the possibility of deployment, but I'm not currently expecting to go anywhere any time soon."

I worry that once again his service for our country will come back to hurt him. If an employer has a choice between hiring an applicant who isn't in the military and doesn't have the potential of getting called away at a moment's notice and hiring someone like Cliff, you almost can't blame them for hiring the other person. But it makes it difficult for a reservist who wants to serve his country and at the same time work to provide for his family.

The other thing that makes Cliff's situation harder is that what he

does in the Navy is not what he's done in the workplace. He's a marketing guy in the civilian world. And in Nashville—in the land of an odd
mix of cowboys and metrosexuals, boots and piercings—someone who
puts on a desert cammy uniform and knows how to do cadences is a bit
out of the norm. Maybe too out of the norm for their taste.

So we keep praying. And we keep asking others to pray. Sometimes
that's the best thing a wife can do.

*   *   *

This week I feel as though we've been living in a blender and someone forgot to turn off the "crush ice" button. Money has been tighter
than it has ever been. We can no longer go to either of our parents—
they've already helped so much, and we've reached the point where we
can't ask anymore. I'm between book projects and freelancing is slow.
Cliff is doing everything he can to bring in an income, and as frustrat-
ing as it feels to still be super tight with finances, I'm proud of him for
the effort he's making.

Besides his Navy pay one weekend a month, he's working these
contract projects as they come up, and he also just took a job delivering
pizzas, the fourth part-time job he's working. I know it wasn't easy for
him to do it. And we've quickly discovered pizza guys don't make much
at all. Most of what they make has to come from tips. And people are
pretty stingy tippers when it comes to their pizza. (I somehow feel this
is payback because I'm usually one of those people.) Cliff's had several
long-distance deliveries where he's gotten no tip at all. But the money
he is making is at least something, and we're trying to stay grateful for
what we do have.

Cliff has been waiting as patiently as possible to hear from the job
he interviewed for. He's called a couple of times just to check in, and
it's always been the same answer: "We're still interviewing applicants,
and we'll be making a decision soon." So in the meantime we've been
praying hard.

It's funny what happens sometimes when you pray. God doesn't
always answer your prayer the way you think he will. The way you
might want him to. That's what we discovered this week.

It started Tuesday night. Cliff was out on his pizza runs, and I was home and had just put Caleb to bed when the phone rang. It was Cliff.

"Sara."

His voice sounded shaky. I could feel the color drain from my face and my shoulders trembled a little bit.

"Is everything OK?"

"I was in a car accident tonight," he told me. "I'm OK, but the car's messed up pretty bad, and I need you to come get me."

I found out later, when he was able to tell me the whole story, that he'd pulled out to turn left on a busy road, and a car coming from the left had been driving faster than Cliff realized. When Cliff pulled out in front of him, the other driver, who was just a sixteen-year-old kid, panicked, and instead of swerving to the right, he swerved to the left, knocking Cliff's car into the ditch. Because Cliff was the one who'd pulled out, he also was the one who got the traffic citation. The police officer on the scene also told him his car was more than likely totaled.

As I got Caleb up and into the car to drive to the pizza store where Cliff was, a million emotions swam through my head. I was so thankful he was OK. But I was so frustrated that we now had no car. Granted, it was a second car, but it was paid for. Now how would Cliff be able to work his pizza-delivery shifts? Or would he even want to? Would he get fired for having an accident in the first place? How much would the ticket cost? Would the other driver sue? The stress of everything was getting to me, and I had to fight back the anger I could feel rising up. This was not a time to be mad. I knew Cliff felt horrible enough.

I pulled into the parking lot and waited, per Cliff's instructions, for him to come out. When he got into the car, I gave him a long hug. He looked OK. A little shaky but OK. He explained more fully what had happened and where the car had been taken, that we'd need to go down the next day and get the rest of his stuff out of it, that he'd had to fill out a report for work, and that he didn't think he would be fired. But he wasn't really sure he wanted to work there anymore, either. I couldn't really blame him.

As soon as we got home, while I got Caleb back to bed, Cliff called our insurance company to report the accident and to find out what the next steps were. I quietly waited by the doorway and listened while he finished up.

After he got off the phone, he said, "I need to call our local agent tomorrow, and then they'll need a copy of the body shop's report and the police report, and then they'll figure out what the car is worth."

His voice cracked, and I saw his shoulders slump slightly. As he took a step toward me, I rushed toward him and put my arms around him as he buried his head into my neck. My husband doesn't cry very often, but when he does, it always reminds me of his gentle side. We cried together and held onto each other.

"I'm so sorry," he said, over and over. "I know this is the worst timing for something like this to happen. I'm so sorry."

"It's OK, it's OK," I said, and I meant it. The frustration I'd felt just a little while earlier was gone, replaced by a whole lot of love for Cliff. If there is one thing I am learning about marriage, it's that the "for worse" part we take with our vows makes the "for better" all that more important. It's the worst parts of life together that make us enjoy the better parts all the more. And it's the worst parts that truly test how strong our marriages really are. And for me, it's important to be strong.

I held my husband, trying to be strong for him the way he is so often strong for me.

"We're going to get through this," I told him, repeating words he's told me before. I had no idea the weight those words really meant.

✳ ✳ ✳

The call came the next day. Cliff had been upstairs when the phone rang, and seeing it was the number he used for business calls, I didn't answer. A few minutes later he was standing in the doorway of my office, his head down.

"That was the record label. I didn't get the job. They're going in another direction," he said.

For the second time in less than twenty-four hours, we'd been hit. It was worse than the feeling of being hit in the gut. As we stood there, arms wrapped around each other, I felt as though I'd been hit by a car too. God hadn't answered my prayer. I wasn't necessarily angry at God, but I didn't understand. All I could think, though, was that it was time to move. We'd been standing in place for far too long. We needed to move forward, whatever that meant, and wherever that meant going.

I took a deep breath and looked into the eyes of my husband. "We need to sell the house," I told him. "And I'm going to tell Dr. Eastman I want to be considered for that position."

Like it or not, change was going to happen for all of us. But we'd at least be together in doing it.

Hello, Unexpected

As terrible as that week was, things started looking up by the end of it. We found out our insurance company did declare Cliff's car a total loss—and issued us a check for more than we'd actually paid for it. Suddenly we had money in the bank, and since we didn't need a second car right now, we weren't in a hurry to spend it. But we did need to start working on selling the house.

Something that strikes me as interesting when I read about Martha 31 is her business savvy. I think women usually associate her with the domestic traits—the sewing and the cooking and the doing. But she was also a great business woman who was confident when it came to selling land and selling her own wares.

I wish I felt as confident in selling this house. We've lived in this house on Kenowick Court for a little over six years. It's your standard three-bedroom, two-bath, but it has a great bonus room with an even greater walk-in attic. I've always loved the walk-in attic. It's so easy to access things or put things away.

I remember how much we wanted to change when we first moved in. The kitchen, a narrow galley with not a whole lot of cabinet space, has always been a source of contention for us, something we always talked about updating or changing. When we originally looked at the house, I was working in downtown Nashville and didn't think we'd spend a lot of time in the kitchen anyway. A silly thought, now looking back. We wanted to do more with the backyard and maybe paint and add some built-in bookshelves in the living room.

But after Cliff came home from the first deployment, we stopped complaining so much about the house. And after he lost his job, we were grateful just to have our house. It's funny how much something means to you when you don't want to lose it.

But now we really don't have a choice. The house has to be sold. No income coming in means we can't afford the monthly mortgage payment anymore, and the money we just received from the car loss won't last forever.

Our situation also has me looking at going back to work full time. Granted, I've always worked from home, but now I'm looking at working on someone else's schedule and not having the flexibility I've been spoiled with the past few years. I have mixed feelings about it. After all, I'm in the middle of trying to be the Proverbs 31 wife, doing all things domestic and conquering the challenges of kitchen and hearth. And yet, in order to have a kitchen and a hearth, we need money.

It looks as though our options on how that happens have come down to just one: this possible job I've applied for with my old boss, Dr. Eastman, who I worked for about ten years ago as a news and media relations director. We've kept in touch over the years, and he recently sent me a Facebook message asking if I knew any young and talented communications professionals who might be interested in a position he has open at the College of Christian Studies at a South Carolina university where he's the dean.

After talking to Cliff about it, I messaged Dr. Eastman back and let him know I might know of someone if he could send me some more details. I didn't hear back from him, and finally, after we found out Cliff didn't get his dream job, I messaged Dr. Eastman to let him know I was interested in the position. He replied almost right away, "If I'd known you were talking about yourself, I would have gotten back to you sooner!"

After talking by phone a couple of times, he's invited Cliff, Caleb, and me to come and check out the area, and for me to go through the formal interview process with the university. Cliff is still leery of leaving

Nashville, but I don't know what other option there is. It's either move for this job or move to Louisiana and move in with his parents. And I'm not sure that's such a great idea if there's no job waiting.

So I've worked to get the house ready. Isn't it funny how your house is never as clean as when you're trying to leave it? I've scrubbed the floors and dusted the ceiling fans. I've polished the doorknobs and wiped down all the walls. I'm vacuuming every couple of days, and we've removed all the clutter, leaving lots of space on countertops and dressers.

And in the midst of all of this, I'm still trying to keep my ministry going. I'm grateful for the ladies who serve on our board of directors and for the women who have stepped up to serve on our leadership team. I wonder what will happen though if I'm working a full-time job. And I still have book proposals that are being shopped to publishers by my agent. Somehow, I keep telling myself, I'll be able to do it all.

Do it all, plus one interview. As I was cleaning and staging the house, I failed to notice my phone ringing in the kitchen. A couple of hours later, I realized I'd had a call from a number with an area code I didn't recognize. Whoever it was had left a voicemail. All it took was to hear the words, "Sara, this is Carrie from Focus on the Family. I was just calling to let you know we'd love to invite you to come to Colorado Springs for a taping."

Oh. My. Goodness. God does have a sense of humor. We may be penniless and very soon, homeless, but I get to go to the Focus on the Family studios! I called my mother, my mother-in-law, my good friend Pattie, and my writer friend Jennifer. I texted Cliff, who had left that morning for a drill weekend. I wanted him and Caleb to go with me. This was not going to be just about me. This was about our family, and I desperately wanted them with me for the entire experience. And as hectic as everything was, I couldn't wait.

But right now my focus must be on getting our house sold. David is our realtor. He's younger than we are, but he's grown up in this area and has done pretty well the last few years selling houses. He owns the house next door to us, which he rents out, and we have every confidence he'll be able to sell ours. We didn't say anything to our neighbors before we put the For Sale sign in the yard. Part of me feels as if we've failed in some way not being able to stay here when we really want to, but another part of me says we need to look at what cool possibilities God has in store for us down the road.

So far we've had only a few showings with the house. Though David tells us a few is actually pretty good considering the number of houses that are for sale in our area right now and that some of those have had zero showings. But I've decided Martha 31 wouldn't just sit around and wait for someone to buy her house—after all, "she sees that her trading is profitable and her lamp does not go out at night" (v. 18). That tells me she's diligent and works hard in everything she does. So that's what I need to do with this house.

※ ※ ※

But before I can do more with the house, we need to take a visit to the university in South Carolina to check out where our possible new home and my new job may be.

We decide to invite my in-laws along. I trust Ms. Nancy when it comes to these kinds of decisions, mainly because she has made really good decisions in her own life. Plus I think she'll be an encouragement to the whole change thing, which Cliff is still showing some resistance to. If there is anything I'm slowly learning, it's that as women, we have a great influence on our men. For good or for bad. Though I don't always feel as if I really know how to influence Cliff. He seems to know me much better than I know him most of the time.

I once read a book about several of the women who served as First Ladies in this country and the extreme influence so many of them had on their husbands and their decisions. They may have been wearing the corsets and the flowing skirts, but those women had sharp minds and knew how to get their wishes carried out. I think it was less manipulation than influence, and much of it was for the good of their husbands' careers, as well as the country's future.

So I'm excited about this trip and hopeful that God will make it abundantly clear this is the right direction for our family to take.

The Horns got here on a Tuesday, and we all piled into their Lincoln Navigator the next day to drive the six hours or so east. The university reserved a hotel room for Cliff, Caleb, and me, and Ms. Nancy and Mr. Ray, Cliff's dad, got a room there as well. The plan is that while I spend the day Thursday interviewing with Dr. Eastman, doing a short presentation with the Christian studies majors about book publishing, and also having my big meeting with the university president, Cliff and the rest of the group will go apartment hunting. It's tempting to think about looking for a house to buy, especially with the interest rates so low, but with our house still to sell and the possibility of a deployment on the near horizon for Cliff, it just makes more sense to rent. My prayer is that we won't have to move with a mortgage payment still to pay.

First up on the schedule after we arrived was Wednesday dinner with Dr. Eastman. He picked Cliff and me up at the hotel and took us over to Sullivans, a place downtown offering big steaks and even bigger desserts. I used to thrive on meetings like this. But now not so much. It seems that too often my husband is the one with me, and not the other way around. He interviewed for one job, many years ago, a job he ultimately got, where they required a meeting with the spouse, and as I spoke highly of what Cliff did and the great man he was, it gave me a warm feeling to see his chest stick out a little more and the smile spread across his face. Our words make such a difference.

It was nice to catch up with Dr. Eastman over our meal. He was the first boss I ever had in a professional position. I was twenty years old when he hired me as news director for the university where Cliff and I were enrolled as students, and he taught me much about writing and communication. He was a big man with big ideas. He amazed me with the quick speed he could throw out thoughts, pretty much for any topic. And he had lots of ideas for the college he was now in charge of. It was new territory to be explored and settled, and that is something we both have in common—we enjoy the challenge of starting something from scratch.

The job sounded intriguing. I would be in charge of marketing for the College of Christian Studies, the only position of that nature in the university. There would be events to organize and stories to write, and I'd be responsible for managing the college's website. All skills I had put to use in the past. The fact that I would be responsible for only one college instead of an entire university was appealing, and I was already vowing to myself that this would be a job that I would leave at the office—not bring home with me as I had done so often before when I'd worked "in the real world."

There would also be challenges. Part of my job would require creating a "Friends of the College" development group to help raise funds for student scholarships. This was something I didn't have any experience with, but Dr. Eastman did. I liked that I could learn some things from this job too.

Dinner went well, and Cliff and I both thought the discussion was good. I'd made a point to make sure Cliff had opportunities to talk, especially since his background was also in marketing, and we talked a little about what he might do. We didn't mention to Dr. Eastman that Cliff might leave for a deployment—we didn't want to take any chance that this job might also suffer because of my husband's service. Our plan was that if I were to start in June, Cliff would stay home with Caleb for the summer and get him settled in school before looking at his own options for work.

After we got back to the hotel, my mother-in-law was waiting for me. While my father-in-law napped, she had taken Caleb out with her and found all sorts of outfits for me to try on for my official interview the next day. Ms. Nancy has great taste in clothes, something I'm still working on. She'd found a nice set of black pants with a grey jacket and black-and-white blouse to wear underneath, or if I wanted, I could wear it with a white dress jacket. With Cliff's nod of approval, I decided to go with the white, and once again sighed a prayer of thanks for my mother-in-law, who always seems to bail me out of jams.

I wonder if Martha 31 ever needed a mother-in-law the way I always seem to. I'm thinking she was probably a great mother-in-law to the wives of her sons. Or extremely intimidating. Maybe a little of both?

The next day went well. The Horns dropped me off at the university, where I met Dr. Eastman in his office, and he introduced me to the student club for Christian studies majors. There were about eight or ten students there that day, mostly guys, and as I shared some of my writing experience with them, I wasn't sure if they were interested in what I had to say or not. I saw a lot of glazed-over eyeballs. But I made it through, and after lunch with Dr. Eastman in the cafeteria, we made our way to the president's office for the most important interview of the day.

As we sat down in the president's stately office, I anxiously rehearsed all the questions I thought he might ask. He didn't ask any of them. Instead, he treated the time we had together merely as a get-to-know-you conversation, and he made it clear that he trusted Dr. Eastman's judgment regarding the position.

As we walked back to Dr. Eastman's office, he smiled and said, "Well, that seemed to go very well." He handed me the official job application, told me to send it in as soon as possible, and said he'd be in touch within a couple of days.

As I stood on the steps in front of the building waiting on the Horns to pick me up, I took a deep breath. I think Martha 31 would do anything she needed to to help her family. I wasn't thrilled that I might have to leave my comfortable home office and spend less time with my ministry, but I did want us to be able to pay our bills. And maybe the new location would be just what Cliff needed to make a new start for a job, though the president hadn't been too encouraging in that department. He'd said the city's unemployment rate was similar to Nashville's.

I saw the Horns' Navigator pull up, and I quickly got inside and gave everyone the good report of how my day had gone.

Cliff was excited too. "We've got a place to show you," he said, putting his arm around me as his mom drove. They told me about the apartment complexes they'd looked at, and they thought they'd found the perfect one. It was four minutes from the university, right behind a shopping center with a grocery store and a couple of restaurants, including a Chick-fil-A.

I prepared myself to like it. This was the deal I'd made with myself. If I was getting the job, then Cliff was getting the apartment. It would be his decision, his opinion that mattered most. The apartment manager was eager to show me the two-bedroom and three-bedroom models she'd showed the others earlier. Decent size with a bigger kitchen than we'd had in the house. The two-bedroom came with a little 6 x 4 sunroom; the three-bedroom came with a patio.

Ms. Nancy was pushing for the two-bedroom. I couldn't imagine getting all our stuff in a two-bedroom, not coming from a three-bedroom house. And what about our office? Cliff would need somewhere to put his desk. Could we make it all fit in that little sunroom space? I was feeling very doubtful.

We went back to the apartment manager's office and talked space and price and deposits. We found out that as an employee of the university, we'd get an automatic $200 toward our first month's rent and that after checking our credit, a deposit fee would be waived. Of course we couldn't do anything until we knew for sure I had the job. I reluctantly agreed to the two-bedroom. We could make do with anything for a while, right? I'll just need to call on my homemaking abilities to make it all work. We can do this.

Almost as soon as we got back to the hotel, feeling good about the job and the potential apartment, my phone rang. It was my agent, Andrea. A publisher had just made an offer on my Proverbs 31 wife experiment. I was excited but hesitant. I had wanted this book to follow my attempt to be a domestic diva. Instead, I was now facing going back into the workforce, and I wasn't sure just how much domestic diva experience I was going to get.

"These days, lots of women are having to go back to work," Cliff said. "And their husbands are out of work. This book may be just what some of them need right now."

I took a deep breath and gave him a big hug. Things seemed to be turning around for us. Finally.

A Wife Goes On

So now we're waiting not only on a buyer for our house but also on news about this job for me. I wonder if Martha 31 ever had to wait. From the description in her passage, it sure doesn't sound as if she ever waited around for anything. But I'm sure she did. Maybe her husband was occasionally late coming home and dinner sat on the stove just a little longer than she planned. Maybe the material she used to make those garments for her household and those she sold didn't always come in on time, and she found herself with a messed-up schedule and time to fill.

I'm not good at waiting. If I make an appointment at the doctor's and I arrive a few minutes before that appointment time, I don't expect (or like) to still be sitting in the waiting room forty-five or even thirty minutes after that time has passed. So waiting on something so momentous as a house selling or a job offer, both actions that serve as catalysts to a whole lot more action, is hard. And the old adage, "Good things come to those who wait," is so not always true. As we've already discovered with Cliff's job interviews.

As I wait for the call from Dr. Eastman, I have to admit I have mixed emotions. For as much as I say I like change, part of me is right there with Cliff. I don't want to leave what's become comfortable to me. I don't want to leave our home. My office. My friends who I seemed to really get to know just in the last year or so.

I especially don't know how I feel about leaving the flexibility I've had for so long. Dr. Eastman assures me this job will be flexible and I'll be able to do what I need to as a mom, whether that's work from home if Caleb's sick or work flexible hours in order to get home earlier. Still, working for someone else requires sacrifices and a little, or perhaps a lot of, lost freedom. Freedom I feel I've wasted, or at the very least misused when I had it.

You know the saying, "You don't know what you have till it's gone"? I'm worried that's what I'm starting to discover. The time I had at home with my husband and my son that I squandered. Neglected. Put in second place over something else I deemed more important.

Don't get me wrong. The things I've pursued haven't been bad. I have certainly felt called by God to minister to military spouses, and he has definitely, without a doubt, opened doors of opportunity for me with writing and ministry both. But did he ask me to neglect my responsibilities as a wife and as a mom to do those things? I know I know the answer to that.

Nevertheless, despite my mixed emotions, I am looking forward to the changes. And so I wait.

I'm thankful, at least with the job offer, I didn't have to wait long.

"Sara! It's Dr. Eastman." His call came the following Tuesday after our visit to South Carolina.

"I wanted to let you know I talked with the president, and he is as happy as I am about the possibility of you coming to work for us. And so, if there are no other concerns or questions that you have, we'd like to offer you the position. Can you start June 1?"

I got the job. And with it the assurance of no more guessing where income would come from. If bills would be paid. We're moving, and we aren't moving just to a new state—we're moving to a new adventure. A new time in our family's life that I am sure has God's hand all over it. It isn't exactly as I thought it should have been—I would have loved if Cliff had been the one to get the job—but if past experience offers any inkling into the new experience we're heading into, God always does so much more when we don't get to plan out what we think.

✳ ✳ ✳

With a job on the near horizon and the house as clean as it can be, just waiting on a buyer, and Caleb back to school after his spring break, I've set about with renewed determination on cooking. I've convinced myself that Martha 31 would use any tools and resources at her disposal, and so I've discovered the latest, greatest thing since the proverbial sliced bread, or maybe in her case, manna. Dinner by iPhone.

I've found all of these recipe applications for my phone. My favorite one is AllRecipes. There's a website as well, but it works out very nicely to have on my phone. I can find recipes by ingredient or by main course, side dish, or dessert. I can change the number of servings I need and the recipes will modify themselves. I can even take the recipes I've chosen and create a grocery list of ingredients I'll need, all on my phone. No need to write out a separate list.

I decide to start with one for fish. Fish is either hit or miss with me. I either get it right, very right, or I get it wrong, extremely wrong. Those are usually the nights the pizza-delivery guy shows up to our house (who we now know to tip well, very well, by the way). But I like fish, and I think it's healthier for us than the usual fare we fix, and so I'm willing to try it again.

This recipe I'm using calls for dipping the fish in potato flakes, along with the standard egg mixture. One tip by a reviewer was to dip the fish in flour first, which I do. The fish came out nice and crispy but not burned, with a good flavor. The wilted spinach I decided to fix with it, much to Caleb's chagrin, didn't turn out as well.

I guess I don't yet quite understand the concept of wilted spinach. I'm supposed to steam the spinach over boiling water until it's wilted but not soggy. Well, I tried, but it turned out a soggy mess. And the Mediterranean dressing didn't go over so well either. Cliff gave it an honest try, but after tasting it, I didn't have the heart to make Caleb eat it. Crispy fish: 1. Wilted spinach: 0.

Since the crispy fish went over so well, I decided a few nights later to try another fish recipe, one I found off the back of a fish wrapper. Italian tilapia. We like tilapia, and this recipe seemed to be a winner. I took thawed tilapia, seasoned it with salt and garlic powder, and then rolled the fillets in a mixture of Parmesan cheese and Italian-seasoned bread crumbs.

I decided to serve this one with fried zucchini, and the whole meal was received much better.

After that, the rest of the week consisted of black-bean pizza, slow-cooked barbecue, and meatloaf muffins, a little beef thrown in for my poor husband who has patiently tried all of these new meals. After the last one, he said, "You know, we don't have to do gourmet cooking every night. Macaroni and cheese and hot dogs once in a while is OK too."

I'm still thinking about the fact that he thinks meatloaf muffins are gourmet. What have I done to my poor family?

Consistency

If I had to mark the biggest difference right now between me and Martha 31, it would be consistency. Martha 31 doesn't ever seem to get tired. Or depressed. Or angry. Or frustrated. She's a person of "noble character," someone who is rare in value. And when I think about character, I think about someone who approaches life consistently. The same positive attitude. The same steady hand. The same joyful spirit. No matter what life brings.

I am definitely not always that way.

Martha 31 doesn't seem to let a crisis throw her out of whack. "When it snows, she has no fear for her household; for all of them are clothed in scarlet" (v. 21). Is it just me or is it just odd to mention snow here? When I think of the Middle East, I don't really think of White Christmases. But this verse does say for me that when something unexpected happens, she doesn't fear. She doesn't fret. She's prepared for the worst, and she rolls with the punches and keeps moving.

I seem to do the opposite when crisis strikes. I freeze. I get upset. I wring my hands. And I moan and wonder what we're going to do.

If God has placed women as a thermometer for their families, I would guess that the temperature I want to be is a balmy 74. Not too hot, not too cold. Just right. Comfortable. Cozy. A place where we come together for support. For love. For life. But my inconsistencies—my moments freaking out or allowing my emotions to knock me off balance—keep that thermostat constantly adjusting. Constantly trying to catch up. And so it's not cozy. It's not warm. It's not how I want my family's environment to be.

I'm not sure I can be consistent right now. I've brought too many things into my life, and something always seems to have to give. But maybe this job will force me to be more consistent. To remove some of the extras I've taken on or at least to prioritize what's truly important to me. Do I want to save the world? Or do I just want to make a difference for my family? Or can I do both?

Whether I'm ready for it or not, more challenges are coming. We got word just a couple of weeks ago that Cliff's deployment with his battalion—the one we were expecting to Afghanistan—isn't happening. This is both a blessing and a disappointment. A blessing because he won't leave for a combat zone. A disappointment because many Seabees, including Cliff, were counting on that deployment for income. Cliff isn't the only one who has been without full-time work.

But just a few days after that word came, we received more news. Another deployment has been planned, this one for November. But it won't be the whole battalion and it won't be to the Middle East. An eighty-five-man team will head to South America to do humanitarian relief work in some of the countries there. And Cliff's name is on the list. Which means just a few months after we get to our new home in South Carolina, Cliff will leave. So not only will I be dealing with a new job, but I'll be dealing with all of it on my own.

I wonder if Martha 31 ever dealt with this.

Cookie Bribes and Other God Lessons

I've decided that with our move date less than two months away, we have to take this house-selling thing to the next level. After all, surely God doesn't expect us just to wait for him to sell our house. No, I'm sure there are things we could do that would make a difference and scream "Buy" to the next family who comes looking.

My first course of action was to bake. I read somewhere once that baking a cake or a pie or bread makes the house feel warm and cozy to prospective buyers. So the next time we got a call that prospective buyers were coming, I made one of Cliff's favorites, a 7-Up cake, and let the yummy smell waft through the house. I placed it, beautifully displayed, on my glass cake stand. But I couldn't decide whether I should keep the lid on or off while we were gone. Leaving it on created condensation on the glass, which I'm sure I've never seen in a copy of *Better Homes and Gardens*. So I decided to leave it off. That would ensure the smell would last longer, right?

Our realtor called later, after the appointment had come and gone. The prospective buyers liked the backyard but thought the kitchen was smaller than they wanted. But they did think the cake was a nice touch. Pshh.

Then I decided that baking cakes was too much work, especially if we got short notice that someone was coming to look at the house, so I went the easy route. I bought cookies from the grocery store bakery and had them ready to lay out at a moment's notice on a plate in an inviting spot on the kitchen table. If I couldn't win them over with smell, maybe we could win them over with their stomachs.

The next couple of visits, I eagerly checked the cookies upon our return to the house. Like a kid looking for Santa, I was excited when I noticed a couple were missing. But still no real bite from a buyer.

So then I decided it was time to call in the emotion. After all, I was a writer—what if I wrote our prospective buyers and let them know just what a deal of a house they were getting? I wrote a carefully worded note that I taped to the front door each time we had an appointment to show the house:

> *Hello! Thank you so much for looking at our home. The furry child greeting you is Sammy, who is very friendly and loves people. Please take your time looking around. We pray this house may be a blessing to you just as it has been to us.*

As many showings as we were having, we still had not received an offer. Usually it was that the kitchen was too small or the backyard was too big. Most people loved the bonus room and attic space.

I decided it was time to get spiritual. Maybe God wanted us to let potential buyers know we were believers. I started turning on our local Christian radio station and leaving the music on when we were expecting appointments. It couldn't hurt to let someone know we were Christians, right?

After two or three more showings with no offers, God finally got my attention one day during my quiet time. It was time to just give it all to him. No more trying to do it all on my own. If God wanted our house to sell, it would sell in his timing and not ours. I simply had to make peace with that. So I did. I prayed and put the house in God's hands. And then I let it go.

And one week later, we had another showing. And an offer. And we closed one week after we moved and just a few days before I started my new job. An answer to my prayer that we wouldn't move with a mortgage payment.

May Showers
of Blessings

This is probably the busiest month we've had in a long time. I'm flying to New Mexico the first weekend in May for a speaking engagement I booked several months ago, leading a GOD Strong retreat for military wives at Cannon Air Force Base.

Then we're flying as a family to Colorado Springs so I can tape my interview with Focus on the Family. We do that at the beginning of the week. We move to South Carolina at the end of the week.

It is really important to me that Cliff and Caleb both come with me. The book Focus is interviewing me about is *GOD Strong*, and it's about my experiences with our first deployment. It is definitely as much a part of Cliff's experience as it is mine. I'm still painfully conscious of what has happened and what hasn't for my husband, and though he isn't the one keeping score, right or wrong, I can't help it. It's important to me that he's there and that he sees it as a success for both of us.

I'm not sure how my Proverbs 31 wife plan has worked out so far. My intention all along was to put more focus on my family, more focus on my husband, and less focus on me. And yet everything that's working out for us seems to be with me. The job, the book proposals, even the interviews.

I'm keeping the house clean, the laundry done, and dinners planned, for the most part. I haven't had any dinner disasters in a while, which must be a record. But I'm still not sewing. I'm still not feeling very "profitable." And I definitely don't feel "noble." I want to be a wife that Cliff is proud to talk about and "praise at the city gate" (v. 31). But I feel more like a wife with her nose to the grindstone. Not a very appealing picture.

And as happy as I am that we're moving into a situation where we will once again be able to pay our bills, a part of me still struggles. It's hard not to feel as though I'm doing all the work. Cliff is still working his contract jobs as they come in, but payment comes slowly with those. He is great with Caleb and helps him with his homework and enjoys cooking dinner. I don't know if it's me or the cultural norms I was brought up with that make me scratch my head and wrinkle my nose. I can't shake the feeling that we're doing this backward. That I should be the one at home, cooking, cleaning, and helping with homework, and Cliff should be the one working and bringing home the bacon.

But do I really believe that? Don't Cliff and I work great as a team? Don't a lot of couples these days both work outside the home? They hand off kids and sporting events and dinner, and they just make it work.

My mom was a stay-at-home mom most of her life. She had dinner ready at 6:00 every night when my dad came home from work. While she cleaned up the dishes afterward, he read the newspaper and watched the news. They'd take turns helping us kids with homework, depending on what we were struggling with. My mom was English, my dad was math. My mother-in-law, on the other hand, worked most of her life. When she came home after work, she cooked dinner and my father-in-law helped the kids with homework. Today, my parents are divorced. And my in-laws have been married more than forty years. Was one way really better than the other?

I hear radio preachers, usually men, who adamantly say the wife's place is in the home. I hear women professionals who adamantly say the woman should be wherever she wants to be. Which often translates to "do it all, be it all." But I also hear women who have realized we can't do it all. That maybe we aren't meant to do it all. And they choose what they want to do. I know women who have chosen not to have kids and are perfectly happy having careers. I know women whose greatest joy is being a mom and hanging out with their families, and they thank God every day their husbands bring in the income and they don't have to.

I'm still not sure where I fit.

Cliff tells me he knew who I was when he married me. Energetic, driven, and passionate about making a difference in the world. But does that passion cause harm for my family? Or is it just me? For years, I've had friends, family, and acquaintances approach me with the same words: "I know you're busy…" I once wore that sentence as a badge of honor. Now I take it as a worrisome sign that I've traded relationships for activity, friendships for a list of goals checked off.

Where does my passion for God and his call on my life, where does that passion connect with my roles as a wife and a mom? Does that passion not count any time there's a nose to wipe or a lunch to make? Or does my passion to make a difference, to follow God wherever he leads me, does that passion need to envelop my roles as wife and mom?

* * *

My speaking event at Cannon Air Force Base went well, though I missed my guys. I was so impressed with the women there. They did a great job on the decorations for the space where we met. Their goal was to create a beautiful oasis in the desert, and so they'd brought in these tables and potted trees and plants and strands of white lights. On tables in the back of the room were delectable treats—a chocolate fountain with cake and cookies and cheesecake bites and other rich desserts. If only I had half the hospitality gifts that were shown in that room that weekend.

Most of the wives on this base don't work. It's located in the middle of nowhere, and like a lot of active military wives in other parts of the country, it's hard to find jobs or keep a career going when you're moving every three years. Some do it, but many try to find contentment in raising their kids and volunteering, whether with a spouse club or their churches or communities.

My host, Susie, and I got to visit with one of the commander's wives while I was there. Alice graciously invited us over for coffee Saturday morning. She was short and slim, with a trim waistline and wavy brown hair. Alice has traveled all over the world with her Army husband, most recently Germany, and she had coffee for us freshly brewed from her favorite German blend. Her house was beautifully decorated, and I was impressed with the little kitchen set she'd placed in the middle of her kitchen, which acted as a perfect place to visit when she had guests as well as an island when she didn't.

We talked about her husband's impending retirement, and her face showed the expression of a woman very satisfied with her life and unafraid of what might come. She'd raised one daughter, and she now took care of their two little white Westland terriers and helped as she could with the other wives. Being an officer's wife, though, left her feeling very isolated. Enlisted wives, women who might benefit the most from her help, were often the most resistant to that help, mainly because they worried that any sign of weakness could be trouble for their husbands.

In her quiet Alabama accent, Alice spoke of following her husband from post to post, often moving all their belongings by herself while he went on to the next assignment. But there was no hint of resentment or annoyance. She took pride in serving in the Army, and she saw her service, her role, as important as what her husband did, though he wore the uniform.

I thought about Alice and all the other women I had met as I prepared to fly home to Cliff and Caleb and the weeks of craziness ahead as we got ready to move in the midst of the quick trip to do the radio interview. Before I'd even arrived home, I talked with a publisher about my Bible study for military wives that they were considering. I'd convinced myself I could do it all. Though all of it looked good on paper, examining everything that was coming up close started to scare me.

I feel torn in following what I believe is God's call on my life—to minister to military wives—but don't I also have a call to minister to my family? I often think of life as seasons, and this coming season seems to be brewing a perfect storm. I may be just holding on for the ride.

* * *

The night before we flew out to Colorado for the Focus on the Family interview, I stopped Cliff in the kitchen and put my arms around his neck.

"I just want you to know that this trip wouldn't be happening without you," I said, looking straight into his hazel eyes. "That book wouldn't have happened without your support and your encouragement writing it. I love you, and I know God has great plans for you and for us and our family."

Cliff bent down and kissed me softly on the lips. "I'm proud of you, and I'm really excited about this opportunity for you and for us. And you are my rock. You're what keeps me going."

* * *

Our trip out to Colorado was a great experience. It was our first time as a family to take in the sights of the Colorado Rockies, and I had to admit, I loved traveling with my guys. Cliff has always made it his job to get me packed for a trip, from making sure I know what I'm wearing to organizing my airline information and speaking itineraries. But having him with me made it a whole lot more fun.

Somehow, though, I can't picture Martha 31's husband stopping in on his way to the city gate (seriously, did he do anything else?) and saying, "Honey, can I help you load those meals you're taking out to the vineyard workers today?" or "May I wrap some yarn for you?" And I'm not even sure Martha 31 would have let him. Me? I'm more than happy for Cliff to help.

Arriving at the Focus campus was a surreal experience. We walked into the reception area and were greeted by a sign that had my name on it. After we met the producer, who took us to meet the hosts Jim, Julie, and John, Cliff and Caleb decided to spend the time hanging out at Whit's End, from the *Adventures in Odyssey* stories.

As I walked toward the studio, I tried not to think about all the wonderful best-selling authors and pastors and speakers who had sat in the same chair I would soon be sitting in. And as John started the show's opening with his familiar voice, I could feel my heart racing as I tried to stay focused on the interview while also trying to take it all in. The hosts asked good questions, and before I knew it, time was up and we were done. I wasn't sure how I did. Some of the questions had felt rushed to me, and I worried I didn't answer them as fully as I'd wanted to. But as I've learned to do with everything book or ministry related, I put it in God's hands. And trusted he would use the interview for his purpose, not mine.

Once we arrived home from our quick trip to Colorado, things got crazy busy. I had already started packing some, but now we had just four days till the U-Haul we were renting would be at our door, and we would load everything we owned into it and drive six hours east to South Carolina to start our new adventure.

And that's when it happened.

Cliff started coughing. And complaining of a sore throat. And fever.

There's a distinct difference between men and women when it comes to being sick. Women fight through sickness because they know they have twenty other things better to do than lie down and be sick. Men just lie down.

The timing couldn't have been worse. Four days before we move, tons to still pack up, and I'd just lost my star quarterback.

When Cliff has gotten sick in the past, I have not been the best of nursemaids. Especially if there's a lot going on. I want him to be like the paraplegic and just get up and walk. But I am not Jesus and Cliff is only human. And right now he's sick. If I am learning anything from the Proverbs 31 wife, I'm going to guess that being kind and loving to my husband when he's not feeling well is a lesson I need to learn.

So I resist the urge to freak out and moan and complain about all we have to do and that he just needs to suck it up and be a man and push past the fever and phlegm and pack some boxes. Instead, I push him gently into bed, pull the comforter up to his chin, and bring him cold medicine and Tylenol and tell him I hope he feels better before I quietly shut the door behind me. And resist running around the house waving my arms in despair.

Six hours later, as I'm packing up the kitchen, I see Cliff walk out of the bedroom with boxes in his hands, heading toward the office. And I breathe a silent prayer of thanks that I have indeed married a man's man. And that Tylenol works really, really well. And that honey gets a lot better results than gasoline.

Moving day arrived, and never have I been so thankful for other people. My mom came the night before to help us finish packing, and guys from our Sunday school class were kind enough to come and help load us. Clay, Cliff's twin, drove up from Louisiana with a Taurus their parents are loaning us for Cliff to use while we're in South Carolina. Cliff's driving the U-Haul, Clay the loaner car, and I'm driving our car.

After everything was loaded and we'd said our goodbyes, we headed off toward our new adventure. We had no idea where the adventure would take us, other than the address already plugged into the GPS. There are still a lot more unknowns than answers. But I know we aren't alone. And no matter what happens, God has a plan and a purpose for all of it.

Our mini-exodus was going fine until we reached Georgia. We'd decided to pull off at a local travel stop for gas and a quick break when Clay called, still on the road. Or more accurately, on the side of it. The Taurus had broken down. My first thought was, *You know, extra cars really aren't that helpful if they don't work.* The apartment office would be closing at 4:00, and we'd arranged for some college guys to meet us to help us move in. We were still at least three hours away. Keeping our schedule wasn't looking so good.

While Cliff tried to find someone to tow Clay and the car to the travel stop where we were, I took Caleb inside the convenience store and ordered two little personal pizzas for lunch. The guy selling the pizzas must have taken pity on us because he gave us a third one on the house. We took our lunch outside and sat on the curb under a tree and shared the pizza with Cliff. Despite the setback, I felt OK. There was no use getting upset. After all, unlike my poor brother-in-law, we weren't the ones stuck on the side of the highway. I think Cliff noticed my unusual calmness.

"You seem to be taking this pretty well," he said, as he hung up for the fifth time, still trying to locate a tow truck.

I shrugged. "We'll get there when we get there," I said, smiling. "I know it's nothing that anybody could have seen coming."

She can laugh at the days to come.

Maybe I'm learning more than I think I am.

Bath Rugs, Compromise, and a Woman's Influence (or Lack Thereof)

We made it to town late Saturday night after finding a tow truck company that was willing to tow the Taurus all the way to South Carolina. Why we didn't think about AAA at the time, I have no idea. But Cliff's parents felt bad about the car breaking down and offered to pay for the tow.

After staying in a hotel that night, we were able to get into the apartment the next day and were still able to have some college guys help us move in, though they weren't the same three who'd agreed to help us on Saturday. As we slowly made progress, moving furniture and boxes up three flights of stairs to our apartment, I was starting to stress at the space and wasn't sure if everything would fit.

About six weeks before, I'd called the apartment manager to see if we could still get a three-bedroom instead of the two-bedroom Ms. Nancy had convinced us we could fit into. They did have one, and now I was really glad we'd taken it. It was a tight fit as it was, even with the storage space we were renting for some of our belongings, but we somehow managed to fit it all in.

With one week before I was to start my new job, I felt the pressure to get us settled quickly into our new home. Some people don't mind living out of boxes for months, but I've always had to have everything in its place as soon as possible. And being in an apartment, the need was never greater. However, as with most things in our twelve years of marriage, trying to figure out where everything goes and how we'll decorate requires compromise.

I don't know if it's because Cliff grew up as a twin or if it's just his generation, but he has this weird way of wanting to have input in *everything*. I mean, I remember the days when my father took a week to even notice my mother had repainted the living room. She had free rein when it came to decorating how she wanted.

Me, not so much. I should have realized that something was different when Cliff actually showed interest in what we were doing for the wedding. While he'll tell you his job was just to rent the tux and show up, he actually had a lot more input than he likes to let on. Some things he didn't care about—like the flowers and the music. But he had opinions on other things, especially the gift registry. Not sure if it was the little electronic gun he got to carry around through the store or just the idea that people might buy what he wanted, but he had definite thoughts on the color of towels we registered for, the dishes, the small appliances.

I wasn't expecting this. I thought this was just an understood thing—women get to rule the roost. But someone apparently didn't explain that to my sweet husband. It took us more than a year before we had anything on any of our walls, mainly because we couldn't agree what should go where. We couldn't agree what curtains to put up and what comforter set we liked best. It wasn't that we argued. We just couldn't come to a decision both of us were happy with. I've talked to other wives my age, though, and I'm not alone. Their men like to have input too. Martha 31 clearly never had this problem.

I don't mind it all that much, though. After all, if I want him to share the responsibilities of rearing our son, then it just stands to reason that he might also want to share other responsibilities such as setting up the house or planning meals. And Cliff loves to help set up—it's the *cleaning up* that isn't always easy for him.

But as I try to stay in this domestic experiment of being the Proverbs 31 wife, I feel a strong desire that I should have—and receive—the opportunity to offer more influence when it comes to how we decorate. Don't I have the woman's touch? Shouldn't I get the opportunity to express it? For most of our marriage, I've relented, compromised, caved. But as Cliff and I headed to Bed Bath & Beyond to shop for some things for our new apartment, I was determined to have the last word.

Cliff and I were standing in front of the bath mats while Caleb ran around the aisles, checking out the display televisions in the center. We'd just decided on a black-and-white shower curtain for our bathroom, and the light green rug we'd had in our bathroom in Nashville wasn't going to work. I ran my hand down a bath mat on the shelf. It was one of those new foam mats, the kind that feels as though you're stepping on a soft blanket but also supposedly dries very quickly.

"I like this one," I said, just throwing it out there. I'm not much of a shopper. I don't think about the little details. Once I see something I think works, I get it and I'm done with it. But Cliff kept standing there.

"I don't know..." he said.

I could feel my defenses shooting up. Couldn't he just listen to me and my womanly sense for once? He walked around the aisle, looking to see if there were other options we'd missed. Stepping back next to me again, he studied the bath mat I had voted on and another one right next to it.

"I guess the question is...is it the right shade of white?" he said.

"Seriously? The right shade of white?"

"Yeah. I mean, we want the whites to match, right?" He held one of the mats up to the curtain in our cart.

The thought that the shade of white might be different never even entered my mind. But it did for my hubby. And this is a detail that both endears him to me all the more and drives me crazy at the same time.

"You know, I'm pretty sure it's the right white," I said, pulling out my choice of bath mat and throwing it in the cart.

Actually, I didn't care whether it was the right white or not. It was going in our bathroom, not the guest bathroom. And it was soft. And I cared a lot more about comfort than look. I was making the executive decision. Be confident, Sara. Martha 31 is confident, right?

Cliff still didn't look convinced. But he went along with it, probably just to appease me. Something all good husbands just learn to do, at least once in a while.

The next day, after taking a shower and getting dressed, he came out to find me in the kitchen making breakfast.

"I like the bath mat," he said. "You were right. It looks good."

Maybe I have hope yet with this decorating thing. Of course, we still don't have curtains up.

Unexpected Moves

Cliff and Caleb helped me move everything into my new office at the end of the week, and I'm all ready to start work.

To say I'm a little nervous is an understatement. It's not nervousness about the new job necessarily, but more about the new challenges I'm facing. Before we moved I agreed to a book contract from the publisher interested in my Bible study for military wives, and I've just found out they want an extremely quick turnaround. Like in a month. The same time I'm starting the new job and I'm supposed to be concentrating on being a Proverbs 31 wife. Not to mention the work I'm doing with my ministry and promoting my newest book, which just came out in February. And did I mention I'm supposed to be focusing on my husband? Especially since we now know he will be leaving this fall for a ten-month deployment somewhere in South America?

I'm not sure what God is thinking. It was pretty clear to us that this job was our only option at the time it was offered. And if ever there was a job to go to after working from home so long, this would be the job because it's working for a man I've worked for before, who knows my work and likes it. Who understands the seesaw pull of being a mom and a wife and a professional all wrapped up into one. Who has assured me I'll have the flexibility I need to run my family and my ministry as well as my job.

But with Cliff scheduled to leave, that means I'll be working a full-time job and being a single mom. Just those two things are enough to keep anyone really busy, and yet I've eliminated nothing I was doing before as I've taken on this new position. But first I have to finish this Bible study. The timing isn't great, but the opportunity to produce a Bible study specifically for military wives is one I don't think I can pass up or say no to. I'm just not sure how I can keep all of these plates spinning. Or for how long, anyway.

* * *

We just got back from my first business trip with my new position. A trip down to Orlando for the annual convention for the church denomination our university is affiliated with. I have been to this conference quite a few times, but it's been several years. Cliff and Caleb were able to go with me, and while I worked the booth for our college, they got to hang out at Disney World each day. Each night after I made my way back to the hotel room, I would rub my aching feet and wait for them to get back with stories of their day. I'm still not used to being back in heels.

When I was in my early twenties, the attitudes within the denomination used to frustrate me, especially during convention time. It seemed like such a boys club. Though you saw plenty of women on staff at all the ministries and organizations that make up our denomination, they always seemed to be the workhorses while the men ran the show, made the decisions, and got the attention.

But still, even with women, there's a balance. I discovered that women expected you to act a certain way when it came to work. Just twenty-six when I took my first corporate position with a Christian publisher in Nashville, I had lots of ambition and determination and wanted to do my absolute best. I wanted to be the best, as well.

I found out quickly that others, especially women, aren't always as happy for your success. My boss, a straitlaced, by-the-book middle manager, liked to give what he called "360 reviews" when it came time for our annual job evaluation. He would give any of the folks you worked with an opportunity to give their take on your job performance—anonymously. That first year, being the young rookie writer who had somehow managed to get the opportunity to travel overseas and write a book, I was slammed by my so-called colleagues.

"Bad writer."

"Self-centered."

"Has a lot of areas to improve."

Their jealous and hurtful feedback cut deep, and I'd felt my wings clipped that day. My boss had no thoughts on their reactions and presented their words as though he were presenting the day's menu in the cafeteria.

From that experience, I learned to keep my joys and my successes and things I was working on away from my coworkers ears and knowledge, including the next book that I wrote as a work-for-hire project. Amazingly, my next year's review was glowing. I was a great writer. I did a wonderful job with stories.

When I finally decided to leave that position and work from home as a writer, I gave as my primary reason for leaving that I wanted to be at home with Caleb. That was partly true, but it was neither the entire reason nor my main reason. When I told one of the men in our office I was leaving, he got tears in his eyes at the thought that I was exiting to take on my natural role as a mother. At the time it offended and frustrated me. Would he have done the same thing if a guy had said he wanted to go home and spend more time being a dad?

I worked hard in my quest to be a great writer in those early days working from home. And while I was grateful to have the flexibility of being with Caleb his last year before he went to kindergarten, now looking back, I know I missed some opportunities to just be a mom. And to be OK with that.

I always struggled to relate to women my age who had gone to college and earned degrees, but weren't doing anything "but" being mothers and raising their families. And yet, I know so many moms now who raise their families and also run businesses on the side, whether Avon or Mary Kay or Tupperware or any number of other opportunities that are out there. And that seems to be what Martha 31 did. She ran her family, but she also looked for opportunities for income.

And maybe that's what this job is. The writing. Maybe these are my vineyards, my wares to be sold. If only I had the confidence she had.

New Adventures,
Old Habits

It's been a few weeks, and I'm slowly getting used to my new schedule as our family gets used to our new home. Since it's summertime, it's a little less hectic than I know it will be when school hits. But I'm trying to follow Martha 31 as best I can, though I still have a lot on the list to get to. Specifically sewing or any kind of domestic creations using fabric or yarn or thread.

But that will have to wait. I'm currently in the middle of writing this Bible study, and to say it isn't easy has to be the understatement of my life. I'm working eight hours a day, I come home, fix dinner, spend a little time with Cliff and Caleb, and get to writing. Not how I envisioned becoming the domestic diva I aspired to be.

The more stressed I get, the more Cliff steps in to help, and then the more guilty I feel for not being the kind of wife who can take it all and run with it. But then part of me thinks, *Well, why not let him help since I'm already doing a lot? What silly rule have I come up with that says he can't help?*

The job is good. It's interesting and I'm getting to use a combination of skills I've developed over the years. However, my boss is an idea guy, and I've started noticing a pattern: when he comes into my office, I better be prepared for more work. Or at least more projects to add to my ever-growing list.

But I confess, we're less than a month into this new adventure, and I'm wondering what I've gotten myself into. This morning I actually stood in my bathroom and did one of those primeval screams, the kind where you throw your head back and your hands toward the ceiling, open your mouth as wide as possible, and just let 'er rip. Except because we're living in an apartment and my husband and son were in the very next room, innocently playing with our iPhones, I screamed silently. I didn't want to scare them or our neighbors. I looked like one of those damsel's in distress in a bad silent movie, letting loose what you know is a horrible bloodcurdling scream, but because there's no sound, it just looks like her TMJ's flared up again.

I stood there, screaming silently, because I have no idea how I'm going to get it all done. I suppose I'm no different from many other women who have difficulty saying no, who sign up for the bake sales and school field trips and offer to lead the office charity event and teach Sunday school and women's Bible study. My problem is that I can't say no to myself, and once again I'm stuck in the midst of writing projects that have logjammed like a bad version of Atlanta traffic.

It's hard to fault the woman who can't say no; she means well, her heart's in the right place even if her mind is a little loose. And if you go by Martha 31's example, it doesn't look as if she said no to much at all. But it does look like she delegated. She had children but she also had servants. Hmmm. Maybe I need a servant, er, assistant.

My mom used to hire someone to clean the house when she started working after we kids were older, and she didn't see anything wrong with it if it took away some stress and one less thing to worry about. I have writer friends who use personal or virtual assistants to help take care of certain tasks they don't want to have to take care of. Maybe my problem is I need to be more organized.

I decide to go the high-tech route. I found recipes on my phone, I'm sure I can find good organizational apps. Of course I do. Soon, I've downloaded an app to help me keep track of chores and an app to help me keep track of lists. Now, what app is going to help make sure I actually do these apps? Yeah.

What I struggle with at the moment is that Cliff is home. He and

Caleb are having a great time hanging out together. Cliff is also work-ing on some contract work, scheduling more radio buys for the client he's been helping. But right now there's a pile of dirty clothes lying in the middle of our bathroom floor. Every time I walk in there I think, *Someone should pick that up.* Pretty silly, I know, since I seem to be the only someone that will.

Cliff might disagree, but I like to think that when I was working at home, I still got the house picked up, the laundry done, the dishes put away each day. I know different people have different styles, but Cliff's style of cleaning seems to be the minimalist style. As in mini-mal amount. When I try to talk to him about it, his reasoning is that I'm just better at cleaning than he is. Yes, because it takes great talent to know just how to rub a brush around a toilet bowl. Or keep laun-dry going and finished in a day instead of stretched out over a week.

Maybe I'm just a wishful thinker, but I keep hoping that one day my husband will figure out that both of us are perfectly capable of doing chores.

* * *

I've decided that if I can't hire an assistant, Cliff can at least help until he gets a full-time job or leaves for his deployment. But I'm pretty sure Martha 31 would not approve. Especially with what I'm about to ask him to do. But I have a valid excuse. Since we still have only one car (the Taurus is *still* in the shop), and since Caleb has summer day camp this week, Cliff's the driver for the week. And I really need mois-turizer. The right moisturizer. The kind that can be bought only from a certain store that screams "woman" before you even get in the door.

"Hey you," I say, as I walk out of our bathroom with my empty moisturizer bottle in my hand.

He looks up from whatever he's doing.

"Would you mind running an errand for me?" I start, but it's too late. He's already seen the bottle.

"Yeah…what?"

He knows he's trapped. That I'm getting ready to make him head into parts most men would scream and run from. It's just one step up from making him walk down the feminine hygiene aisle at the grocery store. But I take a deep breath and keep going.

"Could you stop by Ulta, maybe after you pick Caleb up today, and get me another thing of this? Just show this bottle and say 'I need a bigger version.' You'll be fine. And thank you."

When I got home tonight, there was my moisturizer, waiting for me. But Cliff did declare it would be a long time before he stepped foot in there again. That's okay with me…my moisturizer lasts a good long while.

✳ ✳ ✳

Today I heard that a news anchor on the national cable news network we watch is leaving. Her reason? To focus on her family. I can't help but feel a little jealous, a feeling that would never have crossed my mind a few years ago. But today it does. I mean, what was God thinking with all of this? Just when I really wanted to be more focused on my husband and son, suddenly I'm back to working full time?

I decide to talk to Stacy about it. Stacy is our office assistant. Her husband is a pastor of a church in town and they have four kids, one each in middle school and high school and two in college. She home-schooled all four of her kids until a year ago, when the second one was preparing to go to college, and Stacy went looking for a job to help pay for it. She seems to handle working fine, though. I'm hoping I can pick up some pointers.

I ask her what she thinks about the Proverbs 31 wife.

She chuckles. "I don't know. I'm not sure I think all that much about her, I'm too busy! I think God calls us where we are and that there are seasons. I loved being home with my kids and I miss it, but I'm enjoying the things I do here too."

I'm feeling a little more lonely in my struggle with this Martha 31 woman.

"But do you ever feel like you're doing it all?" I ask.

"Sometimes," she says, leaning her back on my office door. "It gets hard sometimes at night, trying to get dinner on the table because my husband is just coming home too from being at the office all day. And the kids will make messes, and no one seems to know how to do laundry."

So apparently I'm not all alone.

* * *

I've decided none of this is working. It's Friday morning. The house is a mess, I skipped out on cooking three days this week, and everything is as disorganized as it can be. I'm pretty sure the issue, next to just having way too much to do, is discipline.

I used to be really disciplined and thrived on routine. But being married to a free spirit like my husband, a guy who likes to go with the flow and decide what's for dinner when he's hungry and what we do this weekend when we wake up on Saturday, has taken whatever discipline I had and made it disappear.

But I notice that Martha 31 is an influencer. I need to figure out how to do that with my family. I'm pretty sure I already do, but I'm not convinced I do it the best way I could.

Right now, though, I need to get this Bible study finished. But after working all day every day, it's getting harder and harder to find the energy to write at night. Especially when I really just want to spend time with my family. But Cliff and I've been talking, and I'm going to put this superwife stuff on hold for a bit. He's agreed to take on all the responsibilities around the house for two weeks so I can devote myself to getting this study written. I've agreed not to say anything should his version of taking on all the household responsibilities not exactly meet up to my version.

* * *

Since we moved at the end of May, we've been looking for a church. Churches here are a lot more traditional than the churches we attended in Nashville, and it's been hard so far to find one we're happy with.

This past Sunday, we actually checked out a church we learned about from seeing a bumper sticker on someone's car as we drove out of our apartment complex earlier in the week. We googled their website on my phone as we drove behind them. Unfortunately, we didn't realize how far the church was from us. We finally got there after almost a thirty-minute ride, just in time for the service to start. It was an odd mix of overalls and drums and electric guitars. The pastor was preaching about marriage and the role of the husband and wife. I prepared myself for another Proverbs 31 message.

I was pleasantly surprised though. He preached from Ephesians 5 instead, directing a lot of his focus on the husband's role in the marriage but emphasizing the equal roles the husband and wife play in the relationship. He talked about the Jewish custom of the betrothal—how the man knew who his wife would be and would bring a dowry to her home and present himself and his sacrifice to his future bride. Gifts would be exchanged; a glass of wine would be shared, a covenant of their commitment to one another. Then they would be considered married. But the man would then leave for usually twelve months. His job was to prepare a home for them, and once that was accomplished, he would return to get his bride.

It was a fresh perspective on marriage, and I asked Cliff what he thought as we left that day.

"I liked what he had to say," he said. "It made me think a lot about what more I can do to help you. I know I don't always do as much as I could around the house."

I quickly pointed out what he did do—helping with Caleb, helping cook dinner, especially right now while I'm trying to finish up this project. But I could tell something had clicked for him, and it was reinforced for me a few nights later when he decided to make an ice-cream run.

"What would you like?" he asked. One of the best things about my husband is his spontaneity for ice-cream runs (or any kind of junk food).

"How about a brownie sundae?" I said, in the mood for ice cream but something chocolaty and chewy at the same time.

As I worked on my laptop, I noticed he was gone a lot longer than

I thought he would be. I checked my phone. He hadn't tried to call. Suddenly, he walked through the door, carrying a plastic grocery bag.

The fast-food place he'd gone to didn't have brownie sundaes. So instead of calling and asking me to pick something different, he'd stopped at the store and picked up vanilla ice cream and a micro-waveable brownie dessert, brought it home, and made me my very own brownie sundae. Much to my ice-cream lovin', chocolate-wishin' delight.

Once again, my husband is full of surprises.

Stains of the Heart

Dirty clothes. That's what Cliff and I got into a fight about this morning. A stain on the shirt I'd put on. I'd pulled out a comfy blue T-shirt and noticed it had what looked like a watermark on my right shoulder. But it's Saturday, and I don't plan on really going anywhere so I don't see it as a big deal, especially since I don't think it's going to come out. Still, I knew Cliff would notice.

Sure enough, he took one look at me and suddenly his face was filled with concern. "Aww, you have a stain on your shirt."

Sometimes my husband's observation skills drive me crazy. How is it he can ignore that the bathroom hasn't been cleaned in weeks or the stovetop has spaghetti sauce splatters all over it, but he can notice a watermark stain on a dark-colored shirt halfway across the house?

Of course he wanted me to take it off right away so we could get some stain stick put on it and throw it in the wash, and for some reason this just ticked me off. Maybe it was because I knew he would say something and he was just fulfilling my wifely prophecy. Or maybe it was because I'd tried putting my hair up with a clip, and for once, just once, it was poofy up front and looked nice, as though I'd styled it and not just thrown it up there.

Whatever it was, something snapped and I stormed into our walk-in closet, and he followed me in. Still fussing over why it was so important to take my shirt off right then, I took it off and with my back to him tossed the shirt toward his face. Angry, he grabbed at the shirt, accidentally hitting the back of my neck. It stung, but not as much as what was now stinging inside. I was officially mad.

I swung around and gave him my best glare. It was childish, I know, but I was so frustrated. I hate that he thinks about laundry concerns more than I do, and that so often I feel as if our roles are reversed.

We argued more—he accused me of always having the last word, which I think is an interesting tactic for an argument, an easy way to make sure *you* get the last word simply because the other person doesn't want to give you the satisfaction of being right. So I stormed out, saying nothing. And I'm sure neither one of us felt like we'd won.

Stupid fight, stupid argument. Definitely not found in Proverbs 31. Though there are plenty of other verses in Proverbs about argumentative wives:

> A foolish child is a father's ruin,
>   and a quarrelsome wife is like
>   the constant dripping of a leaky roof.
>   (19:13)

> Better to live on a corner of the roof
>   than share a house with a quarrelsome wife.
>   (25:24)

> Better to live in a desert
>   than with a quarrelsome and ill-tempered wife.
>   (21:19)

The thought that my angry words might force Cliff out on a roof rather than be with me makes me want to crawl under a rock. That is not the kind of wife I want to be. In fact, it's very much the opposite. The wife I want to be resembles another wife I once knew. Her name is Carol, and she's the wife of a photographer I worked with. I'll never forget walking off the plane from a five-day assignment and watching Carol, this grown woman with three kids in high school and middle school, jump up and down, clapping her hands and wearing the biggest grin as she cheered the fact her husband was home and rushed into his arms. The excitement she had at seeing her husband was palpable, and though he said no words, you could tell her joy in seeing him ignited something in him.

That's what I want to be for Cliff—an igniter, not a detractor. I'm not there yet, but I will be.

* * *

Today I'm feeling guilty. Caleb walked in this morning to say, "Happy Fourth of July, Mom." I haven't done anything or planned anything. Cliff's barbecuing some chicken, but that's the extent of our festivities. Mainly because I'm behind on my writing and I have to write. This isn't what I wanted. I was supposed to be focused on them, my family, not holed up in the office yet another summer writing my life away.

But I was the one who wanted to do this Bible study, and unfortunately for me, it happened at the same time my new job did. I should have said no to something. I think way too highly of myself sometimes. A lot of women have the opposite reaction—the "I can't do that" reaction—and so they never do anything. Me, I think "of course I can do that." And then I feel my wheels spinning because I've packed too much into the trunk to move.

I'm tired and frustrated. Pretty sure Martha 31 never put herself in this position.

Cliff has officially taken over house duties while I wrap up this Bible study. I had to chuckle in order not to cringe; his way of being organized was to buy a take-out menu organizer. He proudly showed it to me when it came in.

"Look! Now we can always know what we want to eat," he said.

Great, honey. Chinese takeout it is.

Back On Duty

Cliff has left for almost three weeks with his Navy Reserve battalion for an AT—annual training—so I'm getting an early taste of playing single mom, especially since school started at about the same time he left. With the Bible study turned in, including revisions, I can breathe a little easier right now and focus on Caleb when I'm not at work.

"Caleb, come get breakfast!"

With cell phone and hair pick in one hand, I quickly take out the biscuits with the other. Multitasking does not always go well for me, but thankfully this week it has. I'm still chuckling over this past weekend. Caleb got it in his head that he wanted to buy a mouse for a pet. Personally, I couldn't see ever having a rodent for a pet, especially after the mice incidents we had in Nashville. But I'm trying to be a great mom, and if owning a mouse might help teach him some responsibility, I'm game.

But I decided a visit to the pet store was in order to make sure Caleb is really ready to own a mouse. So on Saturday morning, we got up bright and early and drove to the pet store. We were about ten minutes early, so while we waited for the doors to open, I looked up mice on my phone, and we read all about fancy mice and the benefits and drawbacks of owning them as pets.

Once the doors were open, Caleb and I went to check them out. He was excited, ready to save up his money and bring home his mouse.

I explained the plan—we'd go look at all the mouse supplies, and he could write down what it would cost for food and a little cage, a wheel, and anything else the mouse needed. Then we'd go check out the mice.

I flagged down a girl who was wearing a pet-store shirt and a name tag that said "Mary." Mary was happy to help us and patiently explained everything that we would need to have a pet mouse. Then she took us to the mice. We'd looked at them through the glass on previous trips, but now she walked us into the locked area in the middle.

"OK, which one do you want to hold?" Mary asked Caleb.

Caleb's eyes suddenly grew as wide as silver dollars. "Hold? You mean hold the mouse?"

I looked at Caleb. "You do realize that if you get a pet mouse, you have to be able to hold it, right?"

Caleb looked nervous. "Ummm…"

"Maybe you could show him how to hold them," I suggested.

Mary nodded and said, "Sure thing."

She quickly picked one up by its tail and put it into her hand. As it wriggled back and forth, trying to escape, she encouraged Caleb to put out his hand. Hesitantly, he did, and the little grey mouse ran into his cupped palms.

I watched his face closely. He didn't look exactly pleased. In fact, he looked more shocked and disgusted.

"Whoops!"

The little rodent was pooping, and Mary barely had time to grab it before Caleb had whisked his hands away.

"Do you want to pick up another one?"

Caleb looked very unsure by now. Apparently, the glorious image he'd had of owning a pet mouse didn't look anything like what he'd just witnessed. I decided it was time to rescue him.

"No, that's OK, I think we've seen enough to think about," I said.

We thanked Mary for her time, and as we walked out of the pet store, I asked Caleb what he thought.

"Well, it was really gross when the mouse pooped," he said. "And I could feel his claws when he was on my hand." A beat later, "Mom, do you think I could go get a Zhu Zhu Pet today? I think I'd rather buy one of those than a real mouse."

And you know, I totally agreed. All in all, I felt good about the day. I thought that Caleb and I had both learned something about mice—that we never want them actually living in our house. At least not the kind that come without batteries.

Scrubbed

It's a Saturday morning, and after the hectic pace we've kept these past few months, the only thing on my agenda today is to clean the apartment. It's easier to "set about" my work "vigorously" (Proverbs 31:17) when I've had a few good nights of sleep.

As I spray mildew remover around the sides of our bathtub, I think about how it feels as if I've had a scrubbing inside as well. A year ago I was very focused on me—my needs, my rights, my life, my desires. And even though so much on the outside appears to be pointed toward helping others, I know that sometimes your best help needs to first start at home. So since I've started trying to think like Martha 31, I think, I hope, that mindset has started to change.

I watch the faint pinkish film wash down the drain and leave the bright white of the tub behind. When I get busy with my work, housework generally falls behind. I've never taken it as a sign of anything more, but maybe I should. Maybe when the house gets messy, it should be a wakeup call that my heart, my focus isn't where it should be.

While I move to wipe down the countertops and the toilet, I review in my head what I think I've learned so far in this so-called experiment that honestly feels as if it's had more failures than successes. The wife is the heartbeat of the home. She serves as the thermometer—if she's warm, so is the rest of the family; if she's cold, so is the rest of the family. And if she's an extreme temp—boiling or frigid—the family will follow suit. Calm or chaos comes from her.

I've resisted this responsibility often. It's much easier to point to my husband, the biblically appointed leader of the household, and to examine what I perceive are his flaws, his failures, his lack of whatever. But ultimately, I'm just denying what I really know—that I have a great role to honor and live up to in my marriage and in our home. The question is, do I embrace it? Or do I run from it? My fear is that I've run from it for a while now. But I'm not running any more.

In Nashville I had just started developing some good friendships, and since we've moved here, where we know no one and the only interaction I have with other women is with our office assistant, I've learned that I've tried to do life by myself for way too long. And I don't like it. Having moved around a lot as a kid, it's become too easy for me to throw relationships away, replacing people with activity. To-do lists. Accomplishments. I may be the only woman in the world who does this, who feels this way, but I doubt it. I think loneliness hits too many of us more than we are willing to admit.

I remember, in fact, sitting with a friend in Nashville at lunch one day and both of us talking about how lonely we often felt. And yet, there we were, two friends who enjoyed being around each other and talking about life and family and God, and we still felt the weight of loneliness. I think loneliness is an emotion Satan uses to stop us in our tracks and prevent us from reaching out and seeing the relationships God desires for us to have. We gain something when we have friends in our lives. So I'm learning that I want to be a good friend.

As I move on to pick up the living room and wipe off the dust on top of the entertainment center and side tables, I think about my ministry and the indescribable feeling of joy I get encouraging other women to grow in their relationships with God. The funny thing is I never ever wanted to do women's ministry. But God had something else in mind, and I've absolutely loved the journey getting here. I don't know how other women in ministry do it, balancing all the responsibilities they juggle. But I know I need to do a better job of it. I'm also learning that many other women enjoy making a difference too. And that I don't have to do it all.

I keep thinking that this season of our lives—this job I've taken on, this new city we've traveled to without really knowing anyone—that it's all designed to teach us obedience. Discipline. Though I'm not sure how well I'm learning the lessons. But I'm trying. And maybe that's all I can really do.

I think I'm ready to jump into some of the other aspects of what Martha 31 does. Time to pay a visit to the sewing and crafts store.

Knitting Face Masks

decide for my first attempt in Martha 31's world of creating garments and "coverings" for her family, that I will start with knitting. I once ghost wrote for an author who was extremely into knitting, so much so she had her own knitting room, which she filled with yarn she found everywhere she traveled. I'd attempted to learn knitting back then but got nowhere. I'm feeling better about it now.

So I talk Cliff, who is now back from his three-week Navy training, and Caleb into jumping into the car with me and riding down to our local Hobby Lobby. This is the only store out of the three or four arts-and-crafts stores in town that actually has a decent assortment of every-thing, including knitting materials. Though I've been disappointed to learn that none of them offer classes in knitting. And trust me, I once took a day a couple of months ago and visited each and every one of them and asked. No classes except cake decorating can be had. Apparently everyone in this town already knows how to knit or has no desire to do it, and I'm just going to have to teach myself.

I find the knitting section and quickly see the teach-yourself kits hanging from the end of the aisle. There are a few to choose from, and I note the titles: "Knitting Is Fun!" "Knitting Is Easy!" and "You Can Knit Too!" I'm still a little doubtful, but I pick one and also pick up a video that teaches how to knit. My biggest problem last time was I had no idea how actual knitting was supposed to look, and trying to knit by diagram proved to be a lost cause. Maybe if I actually see a living, breathing person in action, that will help.

The next step is finding yarn. I'm not really sure where to start. Cliff likes this part of the search because he assumes whatever I make is going to be for him. It is, but I still chuckle at his assumption. I'm not as picky about the color as I am about the texture: it has to be really soft. I've never been big on wearing knitted sweaters because they usually feel like sandpaper. I quickly discover, though, that the softer the yarn, the more expensive it is. I decide to go with one skein of this combination color yarn, a mix of blues and grays and tans. I'm planning for a scarf, but I'm going to consider it a success if I can even get the yarn around the needle.

I get home with my new purchase and eagerly pull out my knitting needles and the yarn and hit play on the DVD player in our bedroom. An attractive woman with brown hair, holding a pair of needles with all sorts of completed knitting projects on the table in front of her, smiles warmly. Cliff walks past me as she gets started.

"Welcome to the *exciting* world of *knitting!*" she exclaims in her introduction.

"Is she serious?" Cliff asks, stopping in midstep to gape at the video in mock astonishment.

I swat at him with my yarn, though I can't help giggling.

"Yes, she is serious. Now go. I'm about to enter an exciting world and I want to be ready for it."

The knitting instructor walks me through how to create a basic slip knot, and even at her assurance that this is so easy, I still struggle a bit, feeling as if all of my fingers have suddenly become thumbs. I pause and rewind several times before I actually get one on my needle. Now it's time to "cast on." This is where I gave up the last time I tried to knit. I know, I didn't get very far. I watch intently as she shows which way each needle goes, and after a couple more pauses and rewinds, I get it. After I finish my first little row of stitches, I excitedly walk out into the living room to show Cliff and Caleb, who are plopped down in front of the TV.

"Nice!" Cliff says. "So are you making me a scarf?"

"Yes," I say, "I'm making you a scarf." I think. Better go look up that lesson on the DVD menu.

For the next couple of days, I practice row after row. I'm so excited as I see one row become two rows, two become four, and pretty soon I've already done ten rows. But there's a problem. As usual, I've been too ambitious, and I'm doing more than twenty stitches across. I don't know why I started it out this way; Cliff's neck is thick but it's not huge. As I add more rows, I'm finding it harder to keep them all neat and straight. I have to start over a couple of times, but I keep going.

Cliff is officially impressed when I have stitched a nice swatch of yarn, a little longer than the length of my hand. And I have to admit, I'm enjoying it. But then I notice that somewhere along the way, I've missed a stitch or two—I think real knitters say "drop"—and these annoying holes start appearing in my work. But now I'm impatient. And stubborn. Two qualities I don't take the time to consider that Martha 31 probably doesn't have. So I keep going. And the holes get bigger. Until I realize I've got big problems because if this is supposed to be a scarf, than apparently it's a scarf for summer, when a breeze blowing through the thing might actually be welcome.

Cliff notices my frown, and I hold up my disfigured knitting for him to see.

"This doesn't exactly work for a scarf," I say, frustrated.

"Oh, that's a scarf?" he asks, innocently. "I thought you were working on a face mask."

My funny husband. Really. Funny.

Maybe I need to try something else.

Hanging with the Guys

After another busy week at work, I am anxious to spend some quality time with my guys. Cliff has been staying very busy helping Caleb with homework and taking care of Navy responsibilities.

One thing most people don't realize is that just because reservists drill only one weekend a month doesn't mean they don't work the rest of the time. Of course, they get paid only for the one weekend a month. Cliff's spent a lot of time working on plans for the missions they'll be doing while his group is deployed, as well as making sure his guys are ready and any paperwork, medical reports, and other things are good to go for the deployment. He's been deep in emails and phone calls and has had to take a couple of special trips down to Atlanta for some last-minute medical checks.

I realized today that Cliff's favorite college football team, LSU, is playing their first game of the season this Saturday. We are not huge football people. We've never been the type who schedule our weekends around games. Cliff will watch every once in a while, but I'm usually off doing something or watching something else in another room. I decide that sometimes it's nice to just do what the guy likes to do, and so I text Cliff from work.

Me: Hey, I saw LSU's playing tomorrow. Want to plan on watching?

Cliff: Yeah, that would be nice.

Me: We can maybe fix some chicken wings, a few little tailgating goodies?

Cliff: Yeah! That would be great!

We had already planned to go hiking in the morning. We're still trying to learn the area around here, so what better way than to go hike a mountain? We're not hiking people either, but hey, I guess this is just the season to try new things.

* * *

We all get up Saturday morning and jump in the car and head to the Upper State region of South Carolina, which is about thirty to forty minutes from where we live. Stacy from work told me about this nearby mountain, which offers a state park with several hiking trails.

I want to hike. Not necessarily to wear ourselves out, but I don't want to be done in thirty minutes either. So when we arrive at the main building at the base of the park, I look closely at the routes. Cliff knows when I'm on a mission and wisely stands back and lets me choose. He's not crazy about hiking. I guess he figures he gets enough of it in the Navy, but he does it because I like to do it. And I'm not necessarily a huge fan of the outdoors—decades of allergies took a lot of the fun out of it for me—but I want us to do something that's physically active.

After looking over the trails displayed in a huge miniature-scale replica of the entire park, I decide we're going to hike one of the longer trails. It's a 3.2-mile hike. I figure the only other thing we have planned today is to watch the football game tonight. We can take our time, and even if we move slow, we'll be done in an hour, two at the most.

Only I failed to realize that this 3.2-mile trek is mostly up. As in steep trails that climb and wind, and thirty minutes into it, Caleb is not a happy hiker.

"I'm tiiirrred," he informs us for the fifth time in five minutes.

Inside, I agree with him. But I put on a brave face. "Oh, come on. We'll walk as slow as we need to and we'll stop when we need to, but we can do this!"

I'm not so sure Caleb would call me "blessed" at the moment, but as his mom, I know I have an immediate influence on him, for good or for bad. I want to be the good. Even if at times he gets annoyed at me. We finally finish the trail and celebrate by taking a couple of pictures. Pretty sure that will be the last time we're there.

Once we make it home, it's time to get ready for the football game. We all put on our LSU purple-and-gold T-shirts and jerseys, and Cliff pulls out the chicken wings we bought at the grocery store yesterday. It had been my idea to do tailgate food, but Cliff seems to be in his element and is already dredging them in a mixture of flour and special seasonings.

I end up sitting on the couch while he finishes them, a little miffed that he's stolen my thunder and not really sure what to do besides just watch. I take solace that he's excited about my offer for all of us to watch the game, which we do in HD. The fact that they win makes it even better.

Running Out of Time

We didn't check the mail until Sunday, but on Saturday, Cliff received his official orders to deploy. He leaves October 8. We were expecting it to be November 1. Suddenly, the time we have left feels like a blip. I'm running out of time for this experiment and it's nowhere near completion.

I'm still not getting up early. I really need to plan and cook more meals. I haven't touched the sewing machine I just bought. And I would really love to hear Cliff praise me at the city gate, or in a modern-day version, talk about me to his friends. And probably the thing I should have listed first—I need to fear God and put him first with everything. This latter step I have done, though not as consistently as I need to. But I've had enough experience now to know how important it is to trust God first and not try to do it all on my own.

I'm officially stressing. And one night as we're standing in the kitchen, it all comes out.

We're standing there making a grocery list, and I drop the pen and just start shaking my head.

"This experiment is one big failure," I say, looking down as I try to keep my composure. "I'm not a Proverbs 31 wife—I haven't even come close to doing all I wanted to do. All I wanted to do was learn how to focus on you and Caleb, how to be there for both of you, and then God moves us here and I take this job and these book projects and I haven't done hardly any of it!"

My calm, caring husband pulls me into his arms, places his hand under my chin, and gently lifts my face toward his. He hates it when I look away when we're talking, which I have a bad habit of doing. Looking straight into my eyes, he takes my hands into his.

"Sara, it's not about what you do, though what you have done has been pretty good, I think. I mean, you haven't burned anything."

My mind instantly flashes to the lasagna cheese I scorched so many months ago in Nashville.

"Yes, I have," I say, tears coming down my cheeks. "I haven't sewed and I haven't ironed," I add, the list of things I haven't gotten to fresh in my mind.

"Well, I was kinda scared to let you do the ironing part," Cliff says, smiling.

He and I both know he's a much better ironer than I am. Comes from his dad putting him and his brother to work ironing in front of Saturday morning cartoons when they were kids.

"It's not about what you do," Cliff repeats. "It's about your heart, and I for one think you have an amazing heart."

"But can you really tell a difference? Have I changed? Have I become a better wife, even if I still haven't learned how to make curtains or bed sheets?" I ask.

"Sara, just for the very fact you worry about whether you're a great wife or mom tells me how much you care. You took this job for our family. Not because you wanted to go back to work, but because you wanted to make a difference for all of us. And I will always be grateful to you for doing that."

He kissed me then, long and hard, and my arms encircled his neck tightly, not wanting to let go.

But knowing that once again and very soon, I will.

Spouse Support

Despite what my sweet husband told me earlier this week, I am still bound and determined to do a little more in the homemaker department before he leaves. But I'm frustrated. So I ask Cliff a question that's been on my mind for a while.

"How in the world do you know so much about cooking, about ironing, about all the things you seem to know that I don't? Did your mom teach you?"

I already know part of the answer. Ms. Nancy has told me often how she used to get tired of waiting on her boys to do something like pick up their rooms and would do it for them.

"I thought I told you this—I was part of the Future Homemakers of America club in high school," Cliff said, as he looks over some Navy stuff in our small office at the apartment.

"Seriously? How did that happen?" I ask, thinking I never had a chance. I, obviously, was never part of FHA.

"Well, they met right after my newspaper club, and by being part of FHA, I got out of English a whole lot."

Which totally explains why Cliff has such trouble with spelling. He can cook a soufflé, but he probably couldn't spell it.

* * *

Cliff and I just joined our first small group through the church we're attending. We had our first meeting in the host couple's house last night, and I was pleasantly surprised to discover that every wife there works. Two are teachers, whose schedules coincide with their kids school schedules, and one works in a doctor's office. I'm really curious to see how they manage it all.

Tonight after dinner, Cliff and I do the dishes together.

"I've been thinking about something," I start as I rinse off a dish and stick it in the dishwasher. "Do you think ministry leaders help their spouses at home? I mean, I think about the faculty in our college, and I think every one of their wives are stay-at-home moms except for one. She's a nurse who works a couple of times a week. I wonder how often they help with laundry or do the dishes?

"One of them told me the other day his wife always wanted to be in the CIA, but when they met and decided to get married, she knew being a CIA agent and a pastor's wife might be a difficult combination. So she walked away from her dream.

"I've told you before, if I could push a button and just be a wife and mom, I would. But if I feel like God's placed a calling on my life to serve in other ways too, how do I deal with that? How do I balance it?"

Cliff doesn't really have an answer for me. This whole experiment was never his idea in the first place.

"Sara, I knew when I married you how passionate and driven you were," he tells me, patiently. "It's one of the things that attracted me to you. I love you and Caleb loves you. You are your worst critic."

Maybe he's right, maybe I am just being too hard on myself. I need to think more about this.

Dog Poo

Living in an apartment complex, I've had to get used to certain inconveniences we never had to face as home owners. For one, climbing three flights of stairs each and every day, usually multiple times. Parking in a parking lot that doesn't always have a space up front. And definitely not least—picking up dog poo when I used to just let our dog run out to the backyard.

There are dozens of dogs around here. And the apartment complex provides these nifty pet stations all around the complex with complimentary little green bags and garbage cans with lids to dispose of the little green bags.

But I've been picking up our dog's poo for a few months now, and I still can't believe how many people don't clean up after their dogs. It's especially aggravating to see other dogs' deposits right on the ground next to the disposal stations. Pure laziness on the part of dog owners.

So lately, God's been nudging me to pick up not just my dog's poo but that of others too. Dried up, hard little whatever you call it. Not sure what he's trying to teach me—maybe just about being humble and never thinking I'm too good to pick up dog poo.

Yesterday as I was out, I saw this football-player-size African-American guy out walking this teeny tiny Pomeranian mix. I felt God nudging me to go talk to the guy, but I wasn't sure what I would say. Sammy, our dog, saw his dog right away, and as we walked back toward our apartment, we headed straight for them. I said hello and noticed the dog had pooped not on the grass but on the sidewalk. A lot. I have never understood dogs who poo anywhere but the grass.

"Oh, do you need a bag?" I asked. The guy was a little sheepish as he said yes. I couldn't tell if it was because he hadn't noticed the puppy doing her business or that I'd pointed it out.

I walked back to the station, got a few bags, and ran back over, stooping down to pick up this little dog's really big, really smelly mess. In my heart I was thinking, *I just want to serve like Jesus to this guy, whether he realizes it or not.*

Right away he said, "Oh, you don't have to do that," but I said I didn't mind. I wish I'd said more. I did ask his name (it was Chris) and found out the dog was his girlfriend's and they'd been living in the complex for only a few months.

I wanted to tell him about Jesus. But I didn't. Instead, after I finished, I just said, "Have a nice day," and walked over to dispose of the poo. I'm hoping the next time I see him to ask if he goes to church anywhere, and if he doesn't to invite him to ours. Maybe he'll consider it if for no other reason than I picked up dog poo for him.

Today I'm thinking about that moment and how often as moms and wives we do the equivalent of picking up dog poo for our families. The jobs that feel lowly. Meaningless. Dirty and disgusting jobs no one else wants to do. I wonder how often I've avoided those jobs for the bigger more exciting things I've done—and if I've sometimes used ministry to replace my responsibilities as a wife and mom. I think about my reason for picking up poo for that guy. And I wonder if that's not also the reason why we do those things for our families.

We reflect Jesus in the small things so our families can see him in the bigger.

* * *

I've read to Caleb every night before bed for as long as I can remember. We started out with Veggie Tale books and *Goodnight Moon* when he was a baby. Now that he's a fourth grader, we usually read chapter books, one chapter at a time, and he's slowly advanced to series books.

Right now we're reading *A Wrinkle in Time*, one of my favorites as a kid, and Caleb's loving it.

But I've been looking for ways I can encourage him to love the Bible as much as he loves other books, and while he sees and knows I read the Bible, I've begun to think it's important for me to read with him.

So a couple of weeks ago I started something new with him. Before we read whatever book we're reading at the time, we're going to read a brief passage from the Bible. I've started in Matthew since that's what his class at church is reading through. The other night when I read about Jesus feeding the five thousand, Caleb was impressed.

"They had twelve basketfuls of leftovers, all from just a few fish and loaves of bread!" I said, explaining that each basket, according to the note in his Bible, was big enough that a man could fit in it.

Caleb's eyes got wide. "God is *awesome*!"

I wasn't sure how long he would like our new arrangement of reading from the Bible, and to be honest, I've been waiting for him to complain. But so far he hasn't. In fact, tonight as we got ready to read, he neatly arranged his pillow against the wall so he could prop up against it instead of lying down as he usually does.

"I think we should sit up while we read the Bible," he said matter-of-factly. "After all, it is God's book."

I think I'm learning it takes only a little willingness on my part for God to do incredible things on his part.

She Provides Food
for Her Family

So far this week I've cooked breakfast every morning as well as dinner. With Cliff leaving in just a short time for ten months, I feel the clock is working against me, and I'm so concerned that if I were to get graded as a Proverbs 31 wife today, I would fail miserably. So I'm doing my best to juggle job, family, and other responsibilities and not necessarily in that order.

But it's hard, and where I used to feel like a pro when it came to multitasking, I'm now thinking I need to go back in for retraining. The pork tenderloin almost didn't happen last night thanks to me forgetting to turn the slow cooker on before I left for work yesterday morning. Cliff was the one who came to my rescue.

This morning I made eggs, biscuits, and bacon. I had to wrestle a pan from the back of the bottom cabinet, which made sounds like a five-car pileup on the interstate. Sorry, people downstairs.

So far, if I were grading myself on this Proverbs 31 thing, I'd give myself a D. And only because I think I'm at least trying. Otherwise it would be an F.

Does a Proverbs 31 wife serve or coordinate? Does she do all the work or manage? Does she succeed with orders or a good attitude? I think it's probably the latter for all. And I think my biggest challenge in all this is myself. I am my own worst enemy. My husband doesn't think badly of me. My son doesn't think badly of me. But I think badly of me. I worry and fret and moan that I'm not perfect. Well, duh! None of us are, so why do I insist on trying to be?

But though my husband doesn't realize it, he doesn't make things easy for me. Some husbands won't ever step foot in a kitchen; I can't get mine to leave it.

This week it was my turn to help cook the meal for our small group. With four couples in the group, we decided to pair up, and my night is with Mona. Mona teaches the gifted sections at three different elementary schools and just had her fourth child. She strikes me as very no-nonsense, probably influenced by her many hours of dealing with small people under ten. She also seems extremely sure and confident of herself, and I get the feeling as we talk by phone in planning the meal we're to do together that she doesn't exactly like sharing cooking responsibilities. She'd much rather plan the whole thing herself. Which makes me even more nervous in my cooking abilities.

But I resist the urge to feel competitive about this. It's small-group dinner, after all. Not a food cook-off. Mona and I decided to do soup as a welcome to the cooler fall weather we're finally having now that it's October. She said she would do a cream-based soup, so I decided I could do a chili. I've made chili before, and I've gotten used to using ground turkey instead of ground beef. I bought the rest of the ingredients from the instructions on the chili-seasoning packet I picked up at the grocery store. I know, probably not very true cook-like.

Our small group meets on Sunday evenings, and with my mind already thinking ahead to the next day and the start of the work and school week, I mentally check off what I still have left to do before we leave for our group tonight. Our poor dog is overdue for a bath. I'm usually the one who does it, but I need to get the chili going so I ask Cliff if he will give Sammy the bath while I do the chili. Giving the dog a bath is about as enjoyable for Cliff as doing the laundry, I think, and I can see the wheels turning in his head before he even speaks.

"I'll do the chili if you do the bath."

I sighed and decided just to be thankful that the chili will get done. I hurried through the dog's bath so I could at least come in and take care of the cornbread muffins. Once again, not very hard, since I was using the box variety. My dad used to stock up on this stuff when I was a kid. The chili simmered on the stove, and the oven timer went off, letting me know the cornbread was done. I decided to slice down the middle of each perfect little golden muffin and place a tiny sliver of butter in each. Cliff walked in to see what I was doing.

"You should leave half of them without butter."

I was instantly annoyed. "Why is that?" I asked as I continued to cut open the cornbread.

"In case someone doesn't want butter," he said.

"And how do you want to indicate for everyone which ones are buttered and which ones aren't?"

He half smiled and said, "That's a bit of a problem, but I still wouldn't butter all of them."

I shot him a look. "*You* wouldn't. But I guess *I* would."

I kept buttering.

Just for once I would like to do something in the kitchen without him feeling the need to make a suggestion. He doesn't do it to be ugly or to intentionally tell me what to do—I know he's just trying to be helpful—but it drives me crazy and makes me feel all the more incapable when it comes to the kitchen.

He went one step further getting the chili crockpot to the house. He disappeared into our second bedroom, which serves as our home office, and I heard what sounded like cardboard being cut. After a few minutes, Cliff emerged with a box with a circle cut out of it that fit the crockpot perfectly. His own little carrying case. If there were a Mark 31, I'm pretty sure my husband could be it.

The chili was a hit at the small group, and Cliff passed it off as mine. Though Mona brought enough soup and extras to feed an army.

The next day, I woke up pretty frustrated with myself. This domestic experiment is one big failure, I'm afraid. I still haven't mastered grocery shopping or meal planning, and I've bought a sewing machine but haven't sewn and I've started knitting but haven't completed my first project.

The Final Week

This was my last week to be with Cliff for a while. I took off the entire week from work so we could take care of all the final preparations before he left. We stopped at the local National Guard armory so I could get my military ID updated to active status, and we were able to get the paperwork filled out for Caleb to get his ID when he turns ten while Cliff is gone. I cleaned the apartment from top to bottom, preparing for the next week when I'll be on my own. And we tried to get in some good family time.

But there was a problem. We found out that Cliff's cholesterol test came back high, and he's been put on a medical hold until it's lowered. He's never had high cholesterol before, and now I'm definitely feeling that I won't win any wife-of-the-year awards. Isn't part of a wife's responsibility to help keep her husband healthy? OK, maybe not completely, but I think I could have cooked more often or cooked more healthy, and his test might have come back with better results. It's never a good thing when a service member is delayed in joining his or her unit to deploy.

Cliff has now eaten more Cheerios than he ever has in his life, and salad, spinach leaves, and grilled chicken. And since he's still home, I've gone back to work to take care of some projects I need to get done.

Caleb has been participating in an after-school organization for kids called Christian Youth Theater (CYT). They're working on a play, a short modern twist on "Little Red Riding Hood," and Caleb has one of the lead parts—the woodsman. But there's a problem. I've found out Caleb's play is the same night I'm supposed to be out of town for an important conference for work. Cliff will be gone and Caleb will be staying with my boss's family. I can't miss his play. But I can't miss what I'm supposed to be doing with my job that night either.

I used to think the women I met who just wanted to stay home and raise their families were crazy, but now I think I'm the crazy one. Who told us we could do and have it all? And yet when I think about staying home, I wonder how great the hole in my heart would be, and I know that whisper would gnaw at me, "There's more for you."

I love my ministry. And my job is what's paying the bills at the moment.

I'm torn, up and down and sideways, and in crumpled pieces on the floor.

Burned Quesadillas

How do you burn quesadillas?

Cliff was fixing chicken, I was fixing cheese quesadillas. I turned on the burner, sprayed the pan, added the tortillas and the cheese, and stood there, watching the quesadilla cook. When I thought it was time, I flipped the quesadilla only to have the shredded cheese fly everywhere.

As I'm standing there next to my chef of a husband, it dawned on me that I've turned on the *wrong burner*. As in, the burner my quesadilla is sitting on is stone cold. Whether he noticed or not, Cliff didn't say. I casually turned the one off and the other on. And promptly burned the quesadilla. I was right there, watching, attentive, and *still* burned it. I'm not sure if it was the pan or the heat was too high or a combination. But it was all too much and I left the kitchen.

As I stretch across my bed, tears rolling down my face, I think that it's been almost a year and I'm still burning things. The sewing machine I've bought is sitting in a corner, because I've had no time between my job, book projects, and life to work on any kind of extracurricular project like sewing. Because, after all, in the twenty-first century, sewing is extracurricular. I will not be naked if I don't sew. I will still have clothes on my body and blankets on my bed. I won't be cold if I don't knit. I know where to buy jackets and scarves and gloves. And I won't go hungry if I never cook another thing. Chic-fil-A is right in front of the apartment. Sundays may be a problem, though.

I realize that I may have approached this experiment all wrong. It's not about the doing. It's about the heart. A man, very wise beyond his years, told me that recently, I think. And ultimately, when you go back and read Proverbs 31:10-21, it's not about the doing for her either. It's about fearing God. Honoring God. Loving God. In whatever actions that pours out as.

Do we have a responsibility as moms and wives to our families? Of course. But our first responsibility is to God. And I don't think we can say, "We just need to balance." Because saying we need to balance implies making things equal. And God is not equal with anything. Or anyone. God comes first. Period. And by placing him first, the rest comes together.

So all these ambitions I had—learning how to sew, how to cook well, even learning how to vacuum properly (yes, that was one of my ambitions), all of them are nice, but none of them are as important as what I do to honor God. How I live my life each day to honor him—through loving my husband, through loving my child, through my commitments to my family and ministry and work. But God has to come first. God has to be first. And what I realize as I'm stretched out crying over burned tortillas is that by worrying and fretting and stewing over all these things, I am wasting time I could be honoring and worshiping and focusing on God and his desires for me and my family and my roles as wife and mom.

Instead of waking up each day saying, "I need to prove I'm a great wife and mom," what if I just wake up and say, "God, help me be the wife and mom you want me to be today." And leave it at that. And maybe that means making simple meals so I don't lose my sanity and stress out (of course, quesadillas are pretty simple, but you know what I mean). But maybe it also means making the right choices in time as well as attitude. Being willing to pick up each night instead of sitting down in front of the television. Making time for fun little sewing projects instead of wasting time watching other peoples "realities" unfold on cable.

I may never be a perfect cook or seamstress or even the most polished homemaker. I may always see another woman who seems to have it together a hundred times better than I do. But if I've learned anything from this experiment, it's that my husband loves me. And my son loves me. And God loves me. And I don't have to "do" so much in order to "be."

Praise at the City Gate

We said goodbye to Cliff on a Sunday morning at the Atlanta airport. It was just us three, and having done it once before for his first deployment, it's a depressingly familiar (dare I say) routine. Except Caleb is older now and understands more, and his tears started this time before anyone's.

"I don't want you to go," he said, holding on to his dad, his eyes puffy and red.

I throw my arms around Cliff's neck and we kiss one last time. He looks into my eyes. "You mean the world to me," he says, something he's told me often in the twelve years we've been married. We'll celebrate anniversary number thirteen while he's away.

I'm nervous about juggling it all. Working a full-time job was not in the cards the last time we did this. And we're by ourselves this time. There's no family around to help, and we've moved too recently for there to really be friends.

Cliff must read my mind, because he leans in and whispers softly, "You are the best wife I could ever have. You are the only wife I could ever want."

Now my tears start.

We take a couple of last pictures together, and then he's gone. And it's just Caleb and me, once again, walking back to the car and the drive home.

The great experiment is over. For now. Now it's time to focus on just keeping it all together until Cliff returns. I will probably make more mistakes. I will probably have less-than-perfect results. But I will do it with love. And I will do it with as much honor and devotion to God as I can. Praying all the way for my husband, our marriage, our family, and our future, which only God knows.

But out of all the things listed in Martha 31's passage, there's one thing I've been wanting to have happen more than anything, and just when I'm convinced it's not going to, I'm surprised.

Cliff has been training in California for several weeks now, and we've gotten used to the phone calls and Skype sessions. One night we're wrapping up a conversation, and he remembers something.

"Oh, hey, before you go, I wanted to tell you, I've been telling all the guys about your books."

"You have?" I ask, a little incredulously. I know Cliff's always proud of me, but he doesn't usually say it, and I'm not sure if he's ever read one of my books all the way through.

"Yeah, I brought a few copies with me and have been showing them off. A couple of the guys are ordering them for their wives. I've been telling them all of the great things you do for military wives. And what a great wife and mom you are to us."

A lump catches in my throat as we say goodbye and I hang up the phone.

> *Honor her for all that her hands have done,*
> *and let her works bring her praise at the city gate.*
> PROVERBS 31:31

I have a long way to go in many ways, but I'm looking forward to continuing the journey.

Epilogue

Some seasons last twenty years and others last for a much shorter time. That's what happened to our time in South Carolina. Five months into Cliff's deployment, I'd had all I could take. It was the perfect storm of working a full-time job while trying to care for our nine-year-old with no friends or family anywhere around, and most people I did come in contact with were oblivious to any real needs.

And ironically, it was going through the writing and editing of this book that brought everything home for me. Figuratively and literally, because I'm writing this from my comfy pillow in the Louisiana home of my in-laws, where Caleb and I moved exactly one month ago today. I didn't want to be so busy or so stressed that it prevented me from doing what I needed to for my son, or from fully supporting my husband (home or overseas), or from ministering to military spouses and women in general. So when my health started becoming severely affected, mainly due to stress, Cliff and I both agreed it was time to make a change.

Those changes involved more than just our location. Today, I am striving to make relationships a priority over activity. Family over functions. Time with people over time with inanimate objects such as computers or smartphones.

Which means I'm spending a lot more time at the ballpark, cheering on our son as he plays on a team with his cousins. I'm his biggest supporter, taking him out in the backyard and throwing the ball around with him after school. The other day at practice, his coach even asked me if I'd been working with him at home because he was seeing a lot of improvement in Caleb's fielding skills. Music to this mama's ears.

I work with Caleb on homework, enjoying the glimpses I have of what he's learning instead of impatiently wondering when I can get back to what it was I wanted to do. I'm making time to get healthy, working out every day while getting to know other ladies in the process thanks to the Zumba classes I'm going to—my favorite kind of work-out! I'm watching a whole lot less television and having a lot more conversations with friends and family. I speak softer to my husband when we get to talk by phone or on Skype.

Living with my mother-in-law, who calls herself a perfectionist, hasn't hurt either. I now find myself not able to go to bed at night without making sure things are picked up and put away. I'm learning her systems and how she does what she does. Though the other week when she and my father-in-law were out of town and I was in the middle of making dinner, helping Caleb with homework, and taking towels out of the dryer, Caleb said innocently: "Boy, it's hard when Nana's not here!" Apparently, I still need to learn her skill of making it all look easy.

Most important, I'm learning what it means to focus less on me and more on God, because when I focus my attention on him, he enables me to focus my love and my patience on those who matter most to me. I'm looking forward to Cliff coming home, right about the time you are reading this, and I have every intention of helping him find a new job in our new home, supporting him and encouraging him in any way I can.

If there's anything I have learned from going through this experiment—which really became much more a challenge of the heart than any kind of domestic diva contest—it is that as a wife, as a mom, as a woman, and ultimately as a daughter of Christ, I have much influence. And I can use it for good and for blessing, or I can use it for harm and for cursing.

I want to be the wife who is a blessing to her family, who is praised and remembered, not for the activities or projects I checked off, but for the smiles I wore, the peace I shared, and the deep love of God I hope I instilled wherever I went. That's my prayer.

As for Martha 31? She and I have a much better understanding these days. I'm not so concerned with whether I'm like her or not. She has her place. Her motivation. Her inspiration. But I have my hope. And that hope is in Christ. His love. His peace. His purpose.

He is all the life I need.

Discussion Questions

The following questions are intended for your personal reflection or for group study and discussion. Page numbers refer to places in the book where Sara talks about these topics.

1. Read the passage about the Proverbs 31 woman (Proverbs 31:10-31). What are your thoughts about the woman portrayed here? Does she make you aspire to be like her? Or do you feel discouraged before you get started? Why? (pp. 13-15)

2. How would you describe yourself as a cook? Are you gourmet, short-order, or fast-food? Do you love it or hate it? What's your favorite thing to cook? Who taught you to cook? (pp. 17-21)

3. How do you prepare to receive your husband when he walks in the door? Do you notice a difference with him when you're happy or cranky? What are some things you might do differently? (pp. 25-27)

4. What is your definition of a homemaker? Growing up, what was your perception of a homemaker? What about now? Do you consider yourself a homemaker? Why or why not? (pp. 29-32)

5. What tries your patience? How do you typically react to things that don't go your way? (pp. 34-37)

6. How do you balance work and family? Share some tips that have worked for you. Have you ever put your own desires on hold for your family? How has this made you feel? (pp. 39-43)

7. Sara talks about the softness factor—when she's kind to her husband, he seems to return that kindness to her. Has that been your experience? Why or why not? (p. 43)

8. Sara mentions several times in the book the struggle she has with being identified with her work. What's your view of work, whether in or out of the home? How do you typically identify yourself? How do you think others identify you? How do you want to be identified? (pp. 45-48)

9. Are there areas of your life you find yourself being selfish about? What are they? (pp. 49-51)

10. How are your and your husband's personalities different? The same? How do they complement each other? (pp. 51-53)

11. Have you ever done something out of your element? What was it and how did you feel after you did it? (pp. 55-60)

12. Who is a woman you admire and compare to the Proverbs 31 wife? (pp. 61-64)

13. What's something fun you've baked? What's your favorite sweet treat to serve to your family? (pp. 73-76)

14. How do you handle being in control (or when you're not)? (pp. 77-79)

15. Sara wonders what she's made for her family that adds value. What do you have or what have you created that brings value? Do you like to scrapbook or sew or cook special meals? How are these things blessings to your family? (pp. 81-83)

16. Does your husband listen to your advice? How do you influence him? How do you influence your family? (pp. 85-87)

17. How important is it to you to be beautiful to your husband? How important is it to your husband for you to be beautiful? What's your definition of beauty? What are some things you do to look or feel beautiful? (pp. 89-92)

18. How often do you pray for your husband? What's a prayer you've seen answered? (pp. 93-101)

19. Have you experienced unemployment in your family? Has your spouse? What was it like? (pp. 94-101)

20. How have you handled unexpected crisis situations? Disappointments? (pp. 98-101)

21. Have you ever taken a job out of need over desire? How did you grow from it? (pp. 103-10)

22. In what ways do you try to honor your husband when you're out in public together? Are there things you could do better? (pp. 107-8)

23. How consistent are you in your housekeeping tasks? How consistent are you in spending time reading your Bible and praying? Do you ever find the two go hand in hand? Why or why not? (pp. 115-16)

24. Do you agree with Sara that the wife is the thermostat of the home? Why or why not? If you had to assign a temperature to yourself, what would it usually be? Why? What do you wish it would be? (pp. 115-16)

25. How hard is it to wait and trust God for something? Describe a time you had to do just that. (pp. 117-18)

26. Sara struggles in identifying her role as a wife, mom, career woman, author. She juggles a lot of titles and tries to make sense of how they all work together. Have you ever struggled with titles you or someone else has put on you? How did it affect you? (pp. 119-23)

27. What are you passionate about? How does this fit in with your role as a wife? (pp. 119-21)

28. Have you ever experienced something wonderful and you worried how it might affect your spouse? Or your spouse did not share in your happiness or felt left out as a result? How did you handle it? (pp. 123-24)

29. How much influence do you have when it comes to your home? What do you find yourself compromising on? What do you wish you didn't have to compromise on? (pp. 127-30)

30. Have you ever struggled with working in a job outside the home and taking care of your family? Describe your situation. Have you ever been misunderstood by the people you worked with, either in your job or as a wife and/or mom? (pp. 132-33)

31. What causes you to feel completely overwhelmed? How do you respond? What tools do you use to stay organized? (pp. 135-39)

32. What's something sweet and surprising your husband has done for you? (pp. 140-41)

33. How do you handle arguments with your husband? (pp. 143-45)

34. How do you welcome your husband home when he has been out of town or away on business? Do you show him a lot of love or just his to-do list? (pp. 144-45)

35. Have you ever tried to learn a new skill? What happened? (pp. 155-57)

36. What do you think about Sara's statement, "We reflect Jesus in the small things so our families can see him in the bigger things." Is this hard to do? Why or why not? (pp. 167-68)

37. What's the silliest cooking mistake you've ever made? (pp. 177-78)

38. Do you think Sara has changed since the beginning of her experiment? What lessons do you think she learned? What do you think she's still working on?

39. What part(s) of the book made you think about your own life as a wife? What are things you do well? What are things you'd like to do better?

40. In what ways is your relationship with God an influence on your life as a Proverbs 31 wife?

My So-Called Life as a Proverbs 31 Wife
10-Day Challenge

Perform your own Martha 31 experiments and record what happens.

Day One

My Experiment: Today, go out of your way to show love to your husband. Make his favorite meal. Call him or text him and tell him why you love him. Resist complaining or nagging about things he hasn't done (or things he has that bother you). Pray for him and tell him you prayed for him today.

My Results:

Day 2

My Experiment: Today, get up earlier than you normally do and take a quick inventory of how your house looks. What rooms feel good? Which rooms do not? Do a quick pick-up and put-away before your day gets started. This is not a heavy cleaning day, you're just putting away the clutter. Do the same thing tonight before you go to sleep.

My Results:

Day 3

My Experiment: Today, think about the ideal temperature you would be if you were a thermostat in your home. What are some things you'd need to add? Take away? Make it your goal today to keep that temperature in your household (spiritually and emotionally).

My Results:

Day 4

My Experiment: Today, take a look at your kitchen. Do your cabinets or pantry need organizing? Is there clutter on the counters? Make time to clean up and get the clutter out! Plan a special meal for your family for dinner and use the good dishes. If anyone asks, tell them it's because you love being their wife/mom.

My Results:

Day 5

My Experiment: Today, make it your priority to show patience with your husband and children. Ignore the little things that drive you crazy and look for ways to be supportive.

My Results:

Day 6

My Experiment: Today, look for ways to be kind to your husband. Write a note to him and put it in his car or on his pillow. Tell him how grateful you are that he is in your life.

My Results:

Day 7

My Experiment: Today, begin making something special for your family. Maybe it's a photo scrapbook or a crocheted blanket or a tablecloth for family meals at home. As you work on your project, pray for your husband and your children.

My Results:

Day 8

My Experiment: Today, take care of the little things. If you see dust, don't ignore it; wipe it off. Spilled detergent on the washer? Wipe it off. Are the towels under the bathroom sink messy and haphazard? Straighten them to look neat and tidy. Look for the little ways to invest your time in showing your family you care.

My Results:

Day 9

My Experiment: Start your day with prayer. Ask God to give you wisdom and a desire to serve your family today in ways he wants you to. Look for opportunities to pray for specific needs for your household and individual family members.

My Results:

Day 10

My Experiment: Today, be confident that God has called you to be the wife he's called you to be. Resist any of the doubts you may often tell yourself. Rest in the knowledge that God has placed you where you are to make a difference to your spouse and your family. Today, make that difference.

My Results:

Recipes

I've included here for your enjoyment (or maybe just curiosity) the recipes I've mentioned in the book. Most of these were found on AllRecipes.com, the world's largest social networking site for food enthusiasts, and are used by permission. Please be aware that some have been customized for my small family of three. Should you have a larger family, you can go to AllRecipes.com, search for the recipe, type in the number of servings you desire, and the site will customize the recipe for you.

May your cooking experience be so much better than mine.

Banana Pudding

¾ cup sugar, divided into ½ and ¼ cups
⅓ cup flour
dash salt
3 eggs, separated
2 cups milk
½ tsp. vanilla
45 vanilla wafers
5 medium ripe bananas, sliced (about 3½ cups)

Mix flour, salt, and ½ cup of sugar in top of double broiler. Blend in 3 egg yolks and milk. Cook, uncovered, over boiling water 10 to 12 minutes or until thickened, stirring constantly.

Remove from heat; stir in vanilla.

Reserve 12 of the wafers for garnish. Spread small amount of custard on bottom of 1½ quart baking dish; cover with layers of each of the remaining wafers and sliced bananas. Pour about 1/3 of the remaining custard over bananas. Continue to layer wafers, bananas, and custard to make a total of 3 layers of each, ending with custard.

Beat egg whites on high speed of electric mixer until soft peaks form. Gradually add remaining ¼ cup sugar, beating until stiff peaks form. Spoon over custard; spread evenly to cover surface of custard and sealing well to edge.

Bake at 350° for 15 to 20 minutes or until browned. Cool slightly. Top with reserved 12 wafers just before serving. Garnish with additional banana slices.

(Grouprecipes.com, based on the recipe for banana pudding from Nilla Wafers.)

Lasagna Rolls

½ package of lasagna noodles, cooked and drained
1 8-oz. package cream cheese, softened
¼ cup butter or margarine
1 egg, slightly beaten
1 lb. ricotta cheese
¼ cup chopped parsley
½ tsp. salt
⅛ tsp. pepper
½ lb. mozzarella cheese, sliced into thin strips
¼ cup grated Parmesan cheese

Sauce:
2 6-oz. cans tomato paste
3 cups water
2 tbs. chopped parsley
1½ tsp. salt
1 tsp. sugar
½ tsp. oregano
½ tsp. sweet basil
⅛ tsp. pepper

In saucepan, combine sauce ingredients, stirring to blend well. Simmer for 20 minutes, stirring occasionally. While sauce is cooking prepare lasagna rolls. Cream together cream cheese and butter or margarine. Stir in egg, ricotta cheese, parsley, salt, and pepper; blend thoroughly. Spread 2 to 3 tablespoons of filling on each piece of lasagna. Starting at narrow end, lightly roll up each piece. Place rolls, open side down, in greased shallow baking pan. Pour sauce over lasagna rolls; top with mozzarella and Parmesan cheeses. Bake uncovered at 350° for 50 to 60 minutes. Refrigerate any leftovers. Makes 6 to 8 servings.

Note from Sara: I usually am lazy and don't make the sauce, I just use my favorite (or whatever's on sale) spaghetti sauce in a jar. Shredded mozzarella also works fine. I almost always have more ricotta cheese mixture than we actually use, so if you hate to waste, you may want to boil the entire box of noodles and make a separate pan of lasagna rolls to freeze for later.

Crispy Fish Fillets

1 egg
2 tbs. prepared yellow mustard
½ tsp. salt
1½ cups instant mashed potato flakes
¼ cup oil for frying
4 6-oz. sole fillets

In a shallow dish, whisk together the egg, mustard, and salt; set aside. Place the potato flakes in another shallow dish. Heat oil in a large heavy skillet over medium-high heat. Dip fish fillets in the egg mixture. Dredge the fillets in the potato flakes, making sure to completely coat the fish. For extra crispy, dip into egg and potato flakes again. Fry fish fillets in oil for 3 to 4 minutes on each side, or until golden brown.

(Allrecipes.com, recipe submitted by: Kimber.)

Wilted Spinach

¼ cup extra virgin olive oil
2 tbs. balsamic vinegar
1 tsp. lemon juice
1 tbs. bottled minced garlic
1 pinch sea salt
1 pinch ground black pepper
4 oz. baby spinach
1½ tbs. pine nuts

In a bowl, mix the olive oil, vinegar, lemon juice, garlic, salt, and pepper. Place the spinach over boiling water in a pot fitted with a steamer basket and steam 2 to 3 minutes, until wilted but not soggy. Toss spinach in a bowl with the dressing and sprinkle with pine nuts to serve.

(Allrecipes.com, recipe submitted by: KNIVESOUT 1979.)

Italian Tilapia

4 to 6 tilapia fillets
½ tsp. salt
¼ tsp. garlic powder
¼ cup Italian-seasoned bread crumbs
¼ cup Parmesan cheese

Season thawed fillets with salt and garlic powder. Combine bread crumbs with Parmesan cheese. Coat fillets with bread mixture and place on foil-lined baking sheet sprayed lightly with nonstick cooking spray. Bake at 425° approximately 10 to 12 minutes or until fish flakes easily when tested with a fork.

Grilled Zucchini II

1 large zucchini
¼ cup Italian-style salad dressing

Slice zucchini into ¼-inch slices. Toss in a bowl with Italian dressing. Place on a hot grill and grill about 4 to 5 minutes or until nice grill marks appear and the zucchini is slightly limp. Serve and enjoy.

(Allrecipes.com, recipe submitted by: Nancy.)

Slow Cooked Pork Barbeque

Please note: This recipe uses pork chops. I used a pork roast.

4 pork chops
1 18-oz. bottle barbeque sauce
salt and pepper to taste

Put the chops in the slow cooker and pour over them a bottle of your favorite barbeque sauce. With your hands, mix the sauce all over the chops, making sure they are coated well. Cover and cook on low for 8 hours.

(Allrecipes.com, recipe submitted by: LARRYEBER.)

Meatloaf Muffins

2 lbs. lean ground beef
1 10.5-oz. can condensed vegetable soup
½ cup chopped onion
1 cup dry bread crumbs
2 eggs
1 tsp. salt
1 pinch ground black pepper
¾ cup ketchup (optional)

Lightly grease a 12-cup muffin pan. Mix ground beef, soup, onion, bread crumbs, eggs, salt, and pepper in a bowl. Scoop mixture evenly into prepared muffin cups. Bake 1 hour at 350° or until the internal muffin temperature (use a meat thermometer to measure) reaches a minimum of 160°. If desired, remove from oven after 50 minutes, drizzle ketchup on the top of each muffin, and return to oven for an additional 10 minutes.

(Allrecipes.com, recipe submitted by: erica.)

Ms. Nancy's 7UP Cake

1 box lemon cake mix
1 box lemon instant pudding
4 eggs
½ cup oil
1 cup 7UP

Mix all ingredients together. Bake at 350° till done. Sprinkle with powdered sugar when cool.

Shrimp Pasta Florentine

Please note: This recipe was originally written for one serving. Purchase one frozen entrée per serving, and increase other ingredients accordingly. I used cocktail-size shrimp when I made this.

1 package fettuccine Alfredo frozen entrée
1½ cup tightly packed baby spinach leaves
¼ tsp. minced garlic
6 medium-size frozen shrimp

Lightly coat a nonstick skillet with cooking spray, then heat skillet to medium. Microwave the pasta entrée according to package instructions. Toss the spinach, garlic, and thawed shrimp into heated skillet, turning frequently with tongs until leaves are wilted (about 2 minutes). Stir spinach-shrimp mixture into pasta.

("Women's Health" 20-Minute Cookbook, Rodale Inc., 2006 [www.womenshealthmag.com/files/pdf/20_MinCkbk.pdf].)

About the Author

Sara Horn is a wife, mom, author, speaker, and founder of Wives of Faith, a faith-based military wives support organization. Since 2006, Sara has encouraged and inspired military wives of all branches of service to seek God's strength over their own. Her desire is to help women everywhere see their incredible value through God's eyes, to know their distinct calling, fulfill their important roles in their families, and develop strong relationships with God.

Sara has written more than ten books, the majority as a ghost-writer or collaborator. As the wife of a Navy reservist, she had the rare privilege of traveling to Iraq twice in 2003 to report and write stories of Christians in the military—the first time on board the *USS Harry S. Truman*, the second time to Baghdad. Her first book, *A Greater Freedom: Stories of Faith from Operation Iraqi Freedom*, recorded those travels and was written with Oliver North, receiving a 2005 Gold Medallion nomination. Her most recent titles include *GOD Strong: A Military Wife's Spiritual Survival Guide* and the Bible study *Tour of Duty: Preparing Our Hearts for Deployment*. *My So-Called Life as a Proverbs 31 Wife* is the first book she's written for the general women's audience.

Though for many years Sara said she'd never do women's ministry, God had other plans, and he has instilled in her a passion to encourage and speak to the hearts of women, reminding them of the hope and strength we have when we rely on him.

She currently lives in the Baton Rouge, Louisiana, area with her son and her husband, who just recently returned from his second deployment.

To correspond with Sara or to request a speaking kit, contact her at sara@sarahorn.com or visit her website at sarahorn.com. Take your own challenge as a Martha 31 by visiting myproverbs31life.com.